MACHINE LEARNING IN ACTION: CODE YOUR WAY TO POWERFUL MODELS

DR.K.ALICE

Made with ♥ on the Notion Press Platform
www.notionpress.com

Contents

CHAPTER ONE

Introduction

Machine Learning in Action: Code Your Way to Powerful Models is your hands-on guide to mastering the art and science of building intelligent systems. Whether you're a data enthusiast, a budding machine learning practitioner, or a seasoned developer looking to expand your skill set, this book is your compass through the exciting world of machine learning.

In today's data-driven world, the ability to extract meaningful insights and build predictive models is a coveted skill. This book empowers you to transform raw data into actionable knowledge by providing practical, code-based examples and real-world applications. You'll learn to:

- **Grasp the fundamentals:** Understand the core concepts of machine learning, from supervised and unsupervised learning to evaluation metrics and model selection.

Understanding the fundamentals is crucial for building a strong foundation in any field. Whether it's science, mathematics, programming, or even life skills, a solid grasp of the basics empowers you to tackle complex challenges with confidence and efficiency.

Why Fundamentals Matter

- **Building Blocks:** They serve as the building blocks for advanced concepts and skills.
- **Problem-Solving:** A strong foundation equips you with effective problem-solving strategies.
- **Efficiency:** Understanding the basics can streamline your work and save time.
- **Innovation:** Mastery of fundamentals often leads to breakthrough ideas.

How to Master the Fundamentals

- **Active Learning:** Engage with the material through practice, experimentation, and questioning.
- **Consistent Practice:** Regular reinforcement solidifies your understanding.
- **Seek Clarification:** Don't hesitate to ask questions when you encounter difficulties.
- **Real-world Application:** Connect theoretical knowledge to practical scenarios.
- **Teach Others:** Explaining concepts to someone else deepens your own understanding.

Dive into code: Implement algorithms from scratch and leverage popular libraries like Python, Scikit-learn, and TensorFlow to build powerful models.

The Importance of Hands-On Experience

Implementing machine learning algorithms from scratch and utilizing powerful libraries is essential for developing a deep understanding of the field. This hands-on approach provides a strong foundation and allows you to experiment with different techniques and datasets.

Implementing Algorithms from Scratch

By building algorithms from the ground up, you gain a comprehensive grasp of the underlying mathematical principles and computational steps involved.

Key algorithms to implement:

- Linear Regression
- Logistic Regression
- Decision Trees
- K-Nearest Neighbors
- Naive Bayes
- K-Means Clustering

Essential Python libraries:

- NumPy: For numerical operations and array manipulation.
- Pandas: For data manipulation and analysis.
- Matplotlib/Seaborn: For data visualization.

Leveraging Powerful Libraries

Libraries like Scikit-learn and TensorFlow offer efficient implementations of various algorithms, allowing you to focus on model development and experimentation.

Scikit-learn:

- Provides a user-friendly interface for common machine learning tasks.
- Offers a wide range of algorithms, including classification, regression, clustering, and model selection.
- Supports feature engineering and model evaluation.

TensorFlow/Keras:

- Ideal for building complex neural networks and deep learning models.
- Offers high performance and scalability.
- Provides tools for data preprocessing, model building, training, and evaluation.

Combining Both Approaches

For a comprehensive understanding, it's recommended to implement algorithms from scratch initially and then leverage libraries for efficiency and scalability. Experiment with different approaches to find the best fit for your specific problem.

Explore diverse applications: Discover how machine learning is revolutionizing industries, from healthcare and finance to marketing and entertainment.

Exploring Diverse Applications of Machine Learning

Machine learning is no longer confined to academic research; it's reshaping industries across the globe. Let's explore how it's revolutionizing various sectors:

Healthcare

- **Disease Diagnosis:** Accurate and early detection of diseases like cancer, diabetes, and heart disease using image analysis and predictive modeling.
- **Drug Discovery:** Accelerating drug development by identifying potential drug candidates and optimizing molecular structures.

- **Personalized Medicine:** Tailoring treatment plans to individual patients based on genetic, clinical, and lifestyle data.
- **Healthcare Fraud Detection:** Identifying fraudulent claims and anomalies in healthcare data.

Finance

- **Fraud Detection:** Identifying suspicious transactions and preventing financial losses.
- **Credit Scoring:** Assessing creditworthiness of individuals and businesses more accurately.
- **Algorithmic Trading:** Making high-frequency trading decisions based on market data analysis.
- **Risk Assessment:** Evaluating investment risks and portfolio optimization.

Marketing

- **Customer Segmentation:** Identifying distinct customer groups for targeted marketing campaigns.
- **Recommendation Systems:** Suggesting products or services based on user preferences and behavior.
- **Customer Churn Prediction:** Predicting customer attrition to implement retention strategies.
- **Sentiment Analysis:** Analyzing customer feedback to understand brand perception.

Entertainment

- **Content Recommendation:** Suggesting movies, TV shows, or music based on user preferences.
- **Image and Video Recognition:** Enhancing search capabilities and content tagging.
- **Virtual Assistants:** Providing personalized entertainment experiences.
- **Anomaly Detection:** Identifying unusual patterns in user behavior for fraud prevention or content moderation.

Other Industries

- **Agriculture:** Precision farming, crop yield prediction, and disease detection.
- **Transportation:** Autonomous vehicles, traffic optimization, and predictive maintenance.
- **Energy:** Energy forecasting, grid optimization, and anomaly detection.
- **Education:** Personalized learning, student performance prediction, and automated grading.

These are just a few examples of how machine learning is transforming industries. As technology continues to advance, we can expect even more groundbreaking applications to emerge.

Master advanced techniques: Delve into deep learning, natural language processing, and computer vision to tackle complex problems.

Mastering Advanced Techniques: Deep Learning, NLP, and Computer Vision

Deep Learning:

Deep learning, a subset of machine learning, has revolutionized various fields. It involves training artificial neural networks with multiple layers to learn complex patterns from data.

Key concepts and techniques:

- **Neural network architectures:**Convolutional Neural Networks (CNNs), Recurrent Neural Networks (RNNs), Long Short-Term Memory (LSTM), and Generative Adversarial Networks (GANs).
- **Activation functions:**ReLU, sigmoid, tanh.
- **Loss functions:** Mean Squared Error (MSE), Cross-Entropy Loss.
- **Optimization algorithms:** Gradient Descent, Adam, RMSprop.
- **Regularization:** Dropout, L1/L2 regularization.
- **Hyperparameter tuning:** Grid search, random search, Bayesian optimization.

Applications:

- Image and video processing
- Natural language processing
- Speech recognition
- Time series analysis
- Reinforcement learning

Natural Language Processing (NLP):

NLP focuses on enabling computers to understand, interpret, and generate human language.

Key techniques:

- **Text preprocessing:** Tokenization, stemming, lemmatization, stop word removal.
- **Word embeddings:** Word2Vec, GloVe, FastText.

- **Language models:** Recurrent Neural Networks (RNNs), Long Short-Term Memory (LSTM), Transformers.
- **Named Entity Recognition (NER):** Identifying entities like persons, organizations, locations.
- **Sentiment analysis:** Determining the sentiment expressed in text.
- **Machine translation:** Translating text from one language to another.

Applications:

- Chatbots and virtual assistants
- Sentiment analysis
- Machine translation
- Text summarization
- Information retrieval

Computer Vision:

Computer vision enables computers to interpret and understand visual information from the world.

Key techniques:

- **Image preprocessing:** Noise reduction, image augmentation, feature extraction.
- **Convolutional Neural Networks (CNNs):** For image classification, object detection, and image segmentation.
- **Image segmentation:** Pixel-level classification of images.
- **Object detection:** Identifying and locating objects within images.
- **Image generation:** Creating new images using GANs.

Applications:

- Autonomous vehicles
- Medical image analysis
- Facial recognition
- Image search
- Augmented reality

By mastering these advanced techniques, you'll be equipped to tackle complex real-world problems and contribute to the advancement of artificial intelligence.

By the end of this book, you'll have a solid foundation in machine learning, the confidence to tackle real-world challenges, and the ability to create impactful solutions. Let's embark on this exciting journey together!

CHAPTER TWO

Demystifying Machine Learning

Machine learning (ML) is a branch of artificial intelligence (AI) that focuses on developing algorithms that can learn from data without being explicitly programmed. Here's a breakdown of the key aspects of machine learning:

Core Concept:

- Imagine a computer program that gets better at a task the more data it sees. That's the essence of ML algorithms! They analyze large datasets to identify patterns and relationships, enabling them to make predictions or decisions on new, unseen data.

Applications:

- ML is revolutionizing various fields:
    - **Finance:** Detecting fraudulent transactions in real-time.
    - **E-commerce:** Recommending products tailored to individual customer preferences.
    - **Healthcare:** Early disease detection through medical image analysis.
    - **Manufacturing:** Predicting equipment failure for preventive maintenance.

- **Transportation:** Optimizing traffic flow and developing self-driving cars.

Types of Learning:

Machine learning encompasses a broad range of algorithms, but we can categorize them based on their learning approach and the type of data they use. Here's a breakdown of some common types of machine learning:

1. **Supervised Learning:** As mentioned previously, supervised learning involves training a model with data that includes both **features** (inputs) and **labels** (desired outputs). The model learns the relationship between features and labels, allowing it to make predictions for new, unseen data. It's like a student learning with labeled examples.

    - Types of supervised learning problems include:

        - **Classification:** Predicting discrete categories (e.g., spam email or not spam, image recognition of cats vs. dogs).
        - **Regression:** Predicting continuous values (e.g., house price prediction, weather forecasting).

2. **Unsupervised Learning:** In unsupervised learning, the training data lacks predefined labels. The model's objective is to identify underlying patterns or structures within the data itself. Imagine an archaeologist uncovering patterns in artifacts.

    - Unsupervised learning is useful for tasks like:

        - **Clustering:** Grouping similar data points together (e.g., segmenting customers based on purchasing behavior).
        - **Dimensionality Reduction:** Reducing the number of features in a complex dataset while preserving important information (useful for data visualization and improving

model efficiency).

3. **Reinforcement Learning:** This type of learning involves an **agent** interacting with an environment. The agent takes actions, receives rewards or penalties for those actions, and learns through trial and error to maximize its reward over time. Think of an animal learning through positive and negative reinforcement.

    ◦ Reinforcement learning is used in applications like:

        ▪ **Training AI bots to play games** (e.g., AlphaGo defeating professional Go players).
        ▪ **Optimizing control systems** (e.g., self-driving cars navigating traffic).

Unveiling the Power: Real-World Applications of Machine Learning

Machine learning (ML) isn't just science fiction; it's revolutionizing industries and impacting our everyday lives in remarkable ways. This chapter dives into the fascinating world of real-world ML applications, showcasing its immense potential.

Here are just a few areas where ML is making a significant difference:

- **Entertainment:** Imagine recommendation systems on streaming services that perfectly predict your next binge-worthy show. ML algorithms analyze your viewing habits and preferences to suggest content you'll love.

Picture this: You're scrolling through your favorite streaming service, and instead of endless options overwhelming you, you're greeted with a curated selection of shows and movies tailored precisely to your taste. No more aimless browsing or disappointment with lackluster recommendations.

That's the power of machine learning in action.

Behind the scenes, complex algorithms are tirelessly analyzing your viewing habits. They delve into the shows you binge-watch, the movies you pause, and even the time of day you prefer to tune in. With each click, like, and share, these algorithms learn more about your preferences, building a sophisticated profile of your entertainment tastes.

From the heart-pounding thrillers that keep you on the edge of your seat to the heartwarming comedies that make you laugh out loud, recommendation systems are becoming increasingly adept at suggesting content that resonates with you on a personal level.

- **Finance:** Fraudulent transactions can be a nightmare. ML models analyze vast amounts of financial data to identify suspicious activity and protect your hard-earned money.

Fraudulent transactions are a constant threat to our financial well-being. From identity theft to credit card scams, cybercriminals are always devising new ways to steal hard-earned money. But fear not, for machine learning is on the front lines of this battle.

These intelligent algorithms meticulously analyze vast amounts of financial data, searching for patterns and anomalies that signal suspicious activity. By examining transaction history, spending habits, location data, and countless other factors, ML models can identify unusual behavior that could indicate fraud.

- **Healthcare:** Early disease detection is crucial. ML algorithms can analyze medical images, like X-rays or MRIs, to help doctors identify potential problems at earlier stages.

Imagine a world where diseases like cancer or heart disease can be detected earlier, when treatment is most effective. This is the promise of machine learning in healthcare.

By analyzing complex medical images like X-rays, MRIs, and CT scans, ML algorithms can identify subtle patterns that might be missed by the human eye. These digital detectives can spot early signs of disease, aiding doctors in making faster and more accurate diagnoses.

- **Transportation:** The dream of self-driving cars is becoming a reality with the help of ML. These vehicles use complex algorithms to navigate roads, recognize objects, and make decisions in real-time.

Imagine a world where traffic jams are a thing of the past, accidents are dramatically reduced, and your commute becomes a relaxing experience. This vision is rapidly becoming a reality, thanks to the power of machine learning.

Self-driving cars, once a concept from science fiction, are now equipped with an array of sensors and cameras that feed data into complex algorithms. These algorithms enable cars to perceive their surroundings, make split-second decisions, and navigate through even the most challenging traffic conditions.

From recognizing pedestrians and cyclists to predicting the behavior of other vehicles, machine learning is the driving force behind this technological revolution.

- **Retail:** Personalized recommendations in online stores are a prime example of ML in action. By analyzing your past purchases and browsing behavior, these systems suggest products that are tailored specifically to you.

Imagine strolling through a virtual store where every corner holds something you might love. That's the magic of personalized recommendations. Machine learning algorithms meticulously analyze your shopping behavior, from the items you've purchased to the ones you've merely admired. This data is then transformed into tailored suggestions that feel almost psychic in their accuracy.

From suggesting complementary items to predicting your next fashion obsession, these recommendation systems are revolutionizing the way we shop. It's like having a personal stylist at your fingertips, 24/7.

These are just a glimpse of the vast potential of ML. As the field continues to evolve, we can expect even more groundbreaking applications to emerge, transforming the way we live, work, and interact with the world around us.

This chapter will explore these applications in more detail, showcasing the power of ML and its impact across various sectors. You'll see how ML is not just a futuristic concept but a powerful tool that's already shaping the present.

Gearing Up for Success: Essential Tools and Technologies

Now that you've grasped the magic of machine learning (ML) and its real-world applications, it's time to equip yourself for success! This chapter dives into the essential tools and technologies that will be your companions on your ML journey.

Here's what you'll need in your ML toolbox:

- **Programming Languages:** Just like any skilled builder needs the right tools, ML engineers rely on specific programming languages. We'll explore popular options like Python, known for its readability and extensive libraries for ML tasks.

Python: The Maestro of Machine Learning

Absolutely! Python has undeniably earned its crown as the go-to language for machine learning engineers. Its simplicity, readability, and extensive ecosystem of libraries make it an ideal choice for both beginners and seasoned professionals.

Why Python Shines in Machine Learning

- **Readability:** Python's clean syntax promotes code clarity and maintainability, crucial for complex ML projects.

Python's Readability:

Python's elegant and intuitive syntax is a cornerstone of its popularity in the machine learning community. Its emphasis on readability enhances code clarity, maintainability, and collaboration.

Key Aspects of Python's Readability:

- **Indentation:** Python's use of whitespace for code blocks improves visual structure and reduces errors.
- **Natural language-like syntax:** English-like constructs make code more intuitive and easier to understand.
- **Expressive power:** Python's rich set of libraries and functions simplifies complex operations.
- **Community and support:** A large and active community contributes to code quality and readability through open-source projects and documentation.

Benefits for Machine Learning Projects:

- **Faster development:** Readable code accelerates development and debugging.
- **Improved collaboration:** Clear code fosters effective teamwork and knowledge sharing.
- **Maintainability:** Well-structured code is easier to modify and update.
- **Reproducibility:** Readable code enhances the ability to recreate experiments and results.

By prioritizing code readability, machine learning practitioners can create more robust, efficient, and maintainable models.

- **Vast Ecosystem:** Libraries like NumPy, Pandas, Matplotlib, Scikit-learn, and TensorFlow offer powerful tools for data manipulation, visualization, and model building.

A Vast Ecosystem for Machine Learning

Python's rich ecosystem of libraries has significantly contributed to its dominance in the machine learning landscape. Let's delve into some of the key players:

Core Libraries:

- **NumPy:** The cornerstone for numerical computations, providing efficient array operations and mathematical functions.
- **Pandas:** Offers data structures like DataFrames for data manipulation, cleaning, and analysis.
- **Matplotlib:** A versatile plotting library for creating static, animated, and interactive visualizations.

Machine Learning:

- **Scikit-learn:** A comprehensive library for classical machine learning algorithms, including classification, regression, clustering, and model selection.

Deep Learning:

- **TensorFlow:** A powerful platform for building and training complex neural networks, offering flexibility and scalability.
- **Keras:** A high-level API built on top of TensorFlow, providing a simpler interface for building neural networks.
- **PyTorch:** Another popular deep learning framework known for its dynamic computation graph and ease of use.

Visualization:

- **Seaborn:** Built on Matplotlib, offering a higher-level interface for creating visually appealing statistical graphics.

Additional Libraries:

- **NLTK:** Natural Language Toolkit for text processing and analysis.
- **OpenCV:** For computer vision tasks like image processing and object detection.

This vast ecosystem empowers data scientists and machine learning engineers to efficiently explore, analyze, and model complex data, accelerating the development of innovative solutions.

Community Support: A thriving community ensures abundant resources, tutorials, and forums for troubleshooting.

The Python and machine learning community is a testament to the power of collaboration and knowledge sharing. With a vast array of online forums, tutorials, and open-source projects, it provides an invaluable resource for learners and practitioners alike.

Key Benefits of a Strong Community:

- **Accelerated Learning:** Access to tutorials, code snippets, and best practices speeds up skill acquisition.
- **Problem-Solving:** Forums and Q&A platforms offer solutions to common challenges.
- **Collaboration:** Networking with other enthusiasts fosters innovation and knowledge exchange.
- **Open-Source Contributions:** Opportunities to contribute to open-source projects and give back to the community.
- **Career Advancement:** Building a strong reputation within the community can open doors to new opportunities.

Popular Platforms:

- **Stack Overflow:** A vast question-and-answer platform for programmers.
- **GitHub:** A repository for hosting and collaborating on code.
- **Kaggle:** A platform for data science and machine learning competitions and datasets.
- **Medium:** A publishing platform for sharing insights and tutorials.
- **Online Forums:** Dedicated ML forums and subreddits offer specialized support.

By actively participating in the community, you can accelerate your learning journey, find solutions to challenges, and contribute to the growth of the field.

- **Versatility:** Python's applicability extends beyond ML, making it a valuable skill for various roles.

Python's versatility is a key factor in its widespread adoption. Beyond machine learning, it excels in numerous domains, making it a valuable skill for professionals across various industries.

Python's Applications Beyond Machine Learning:

- **Data Science:** Handling large datasets, statistical analysis, and data visualization.
- **Web Development:** Building dynamic web applications using frameworks like Django and Flask.
- **Automation:** Automating repetitive tasks, scripting, and system administration.
- **Scientific Computing:** Performing complex calculations and simulations in fields like physics, chemistry, and engineering.
- **Natural Language Processing (NLP):** Text analysis, sentiment analysis, and language translation.
- **Game Development:** Creating interactive games using libraries like Pygame.
- **Financial Analysis:** Building trading algorithms, risk modeling, and portfolio management.

Benefits of Python's Versatility:

- **Increased job opportunities:** A wider range of potential roles.
- **Enhanced problem-solving skills:** Applying Python to diverse challenges.
- **Improved career growth:** Adaptability to changing industry trends.
- **Cost-effective:** A single language for multiple tasks reduces training and development costs.

By mastering Python, individuals can position themselves as valuable assets in a rapidly evolving job market.

- **Machine Learning Frameworks:** Imagine having pre-built tools to create complex structures. Machine learning frameworks, like TensorFlow or PyTorch, provide a foundation for building and training your models. These frameworks handle many of the underlying complexities, allowing you to focus on the core concepts.

Machine learning frameworks are like pre-built construction kits for data scientists. They provide a solid foundation of tools and functions, allowing you to focus on the creative aspects of model building rather than reinventing the wheel.

TensorFlow and **PyTorch** are two of the most popular frameworks, offering different strengths and approaches. TensorFlow excels in large-scale deployments and complex neural networks, while PyTorch is often praised for its flexibility and ease of use.

Other notable frameworks include:

- **Scikit-learn:** For traditional machine learning algorithms
- **Keras:** A high-level API built on top of TensorFlow or Theano
- **MXNet:** Known for its efficiency and scalability
- **JAX:** A relatively new framework with a focus on automatic differentiation

By mastering these frameworks, you'll be equipped to tackle a wide range of machine learning challenges and build cutting-edge applications.

- **Data Tools:** The success of ML hinges on data. This chapter will introduce you to essential data analysis and manipulation tools. You'll learn how to clean, prepare, and explore your data to ensure your models have the best foundation for learning.

Data is the cornerstone of any successful machine learning project. Without clean, well-prepared data, even the most sophisticated models will struggle to deliver accurate results.

This chapter will equip you with the essential tools and techniques to transform raw data into a valuable asset. You'll learn how to:

- **Import data:** Load data from various sources like CSV, Excel, databases, and APIs.

Importing data is the crucial first step in any machine learning project. Python offers a rich ecosystem of libraries to handle various data sources efficiently.

Common Data Sources and Libraries

- **CSV and Excel:**
  - **Pandas:** The go-to library for loading CSV and Excel files into DataFrames.
  - **Openpyxl:** For more complex Excel file interactions.
- **Databases:**
  - **SQLAlchemy:** Versatile ORM for interacting with various databases (SQLAlchemy dialects).
  - **pandas-sql:** Integrates SQL-like operations with Pandas DataFrames.
- **APIs:**
  - **Requests:** For making HTTP requests to retrieve data from APIs.
  - **JSON:** For parsing JSON responses.

Data Cleaning and Preprocessing

Once data is imported, it often requires cleaning and preprocessing:

- **Handling missing values:** Fill, drop, or impute missing data.
- **Data type conversions:** Ensure data types are correct (e.g., converting text to numerical values).
- **Outlier detection and handling:** Identify and treat outliers.
- **Feature scaling:** Normalize or standardize features.

  Pandas is particularly useful for these tasks.

Additional Considerations

- **Data Quality:** Assess data accuracy, consistency, and completeness.

Data Quality: The Cornerstone of Reliable Insights

Data quality is paramount in machine learning. Inaccurate, incomplete, or inconsistent data can lead to erroneous models and misleading results. Let's delve into the key dimensions of data quality:

Accuracy

- **Definition:** The degree to which data correctly reflects the real world.
- **Techniques:**
  - Compare data against trusted sources or known values.
  - Statistical outlier detection.

- Data profiling to identify inconsistencies.

Completeness

- **Definition:** The degree to which data is available and present.
- **Techniques:**
  - Identify missing values and handle them appropriately (imputation, deletion).
  - Analyze data completeness against predefined rules or standards.

Consistency

- **Definition:** The degree to which data is uniform and adheres to defined standards.
- **Techniques:**
  - Check for data format consistency (e.g., date, currency).
  - Identify and resolve duplicate records.
  - Validate data against business rules.

Additional Considerations

- **Timeliness:** Data should be up-to-date for accurate insights.
- **Validity:** Data should conform to defined business rules and formats.
- **Uniqueness:** Avoid duplicate records.

Tools and Techniques

- **Data profiling:** Generate summary statistics and identify anomalies.
- **Data cleaning:** Handle missing values, outliers, and inconsistencies.
- **Data validation:** Verify data against business rules and constraints.
- **Data standardization:** Ensure consistent data formats and units.

By investing time in data quality, you significantly improve the chances of building robust and reliable machine learning models.

Data Volume: Handle large datasets efficiently using techniques like chunking or sampling.

Handling Large Datasets Efficiently

Dealing with massive datasets is a common challenge in machine learning. Employing efficient techniques is crucial for effective analysis and model training.

Key Techniques for Handling Large Datasets

- **Sampling:**
    - **Random sampling:** Selecting a subset of data randomly.
    - **Stratified sampling:** Ensuring representation of different categories within the dataset.
    - **Importance sampling:** Weighting samples based on their importance.
- **Chunking:**

  - Processing data in smaller batches to manage memory constraints.
  - Iterating over chunks for training or analysis.

- **Data Compression:**

  - Reducing data size without significant information loss.
  - Techniques like gzip, zip, or specialized compression algorithms.

- **Distributed Computing:**

  - Distributing computations across multiple machines or cores.
  - Frameworks like Apache Spark for large-scale data processing.

- **Out-of-Core Algorithms:**

  - Processing data directly from disk without loading it entirely into memory.
  - Algorithms like incremental learning or online learning.

Considerations for Large Datasets

- **Hardware:** Sufficient RAM, storage, and processing power are essential.
- **Data Format:** Efficient data formats like Parquet or Feather can improve performance.
- **Algorithm Choice:** Select algorithms that handle large datasets efficiently (e.g., decision trees, random forests).
- **Feature Engineering:** Carefully select and engineer features to reduce dimensionality.

By combining these techniques and carefully considering the specific dataset and computational resources, you can effectively handle large datasets and extract valuable insights.

Data Format: Convert data to a suitable format for analysis (e.g., NumPy arrays).

Choosing the right data format is crucial for efficient machine learning model development. NumPy arrays are often the preferred format due to their optimized performance for numerical computations.

Considerations for Format Selection

- **Data size:** For large datasets, consider memory efficiency and performance implications.
- **Data type:** Ensure the chosen format supports the data types in your dataset.
- **Library compatibility:** Select a format that is compatible with your machine learning libraries.

Additional Formats

- **HDF5:** Efficiently store large datasets with complex hierarchies.
- **Parquet:** Columnar format optimized for data compression and query performance.
- **Feather:** High-performance in-memory format for Pandas DataFrames.

By carefully selecting the appropriate data format, you can optimize your machine learning pipeline for performance and efficiency.

By mastering data import and preprocessing, you lay a solid foundation for building accurate and reliable machine learning models.

- **Explore data:** Uncover patterns, trends, and anomalies through visualization and summary statistics.
- **Clean data:** Handle missing values, outliers, inconsistencies, and duplicates.
- **Prepare data:** Transform data into a suitable format for machine learning algorithms, including feature scaling, encoding, and splitting data into training and test sets.

By mastering these data wrangling skills, you'll lay a solid foundation for building effective machine learning models.

Hardware: While powerful computers aren't always a necessity for beginners, understanding the role of hardware is crucial. We'll discuss different processing options, like CPUs and GPUs, and how they impact the training speed and complexity of your models.

While you can certainly start your machine learning journey with a modest setup, understanding the role of hardware becomes increasingly important as you tackle more complex projects.

Key components:

CPUs (Central Processing Units)

- **General-purpose processors** capable of handling a wide range of tasks.
- Excel at sequential operations and tasks with complex logic.
- Suitable for smaller datasets and simpler models.

GPUs (Graphics Processing Units)

- **Specialized processors** originally designed for handling graphics but now excel at parallel computations.

- Ideal for handling large datasets and complex models, especially deep learning.
- Offer significant speedups compared to CPUs for many ML tasks.

TPUs (Tensor Processing Units)

- **Specialized hardware accelerators** designed specifically for machine learning workloads.
- Offer even greater performance gains compared to GPUs for certain types of models.
- Primarily used in large-scale, cloud-based environments.

RAM (Random Access Memory)

- **Short-term memory** for storing data the CPU actively uses.
- Sufficient RAM is essential for smooth performance, especially when handling large datasets.
- **Cloud Platforms:** Cloud computing offers a vast amount of processing power and storage, making it ideal for large-scale ML projects. We'll explore different cloud platforms that cater to machine learning needs and offer resources to get you started.

Cloud computing has revolutionized the way we approach machine learning. By offering scalable computing resources, vast storage options, and pre-built tools, cloud platforms have made it easier than ever to develop and deploy complex models.

Let's explore some of the major players in the cloud computing landscape:

Key Cloud Platforms for Machine Learning

- **Amazon Web Services (AWS):** Offers a comprehensive suite of services, including SageMaker for building, training, and deploying ML models.
- **Google Cloud Platform (GCP):** Provides powerful tools for data engineering, machine learning, and AI, with a focus on scalability and performance.
- **Microsoft Azure:** Offers a hybrid approach, combining on-premises and cloud-based solutions, with a strong focus on enterprise applications.
- **IBM Cloud:** Provides a range of cognitive computing services, including Watson Studio for data science and machine learning.

Benefits of Using Cloud Platforms

- **Scalability:** Easily adjust resources based on project needs.
- **Cost-Efficiency:** Pay only for what you use, avoiding upfront hardware investments.
- **Speed:** Access powerful computing resources and pre-trained models quickly.
- **Collaboration:** Enable teams to work together seamlessly on large-scale projects.

This chapter won't just list the tools; it will explain their purpose and how they work together in the ML development process. We'll provide resources and recommendations to help you choose the right tools for your specific learning goals.

CHAPTER THREE

Building Blocks: Understanding Data and Algorithms

Machine learning (ML) is like a skilled chef – its success depends on both the quality of ingredients (data) and the chosen recipe (algorithm). This chapter dives into these fundamental building blocks, providing a solid foundation for your ML journey.

- **Data: The Fuel for Learning:** Imagine trying to cook a delicious meal without any ingredients. In ML, data is just as crucial. We'll explore different types of data, like numerical, categorical, and text, used to train models. You'll learn about data collection techniques and the importance of data quality for achieving reliable results.

Data is the lifeblood of machine learning. Just as a chef needs the right ingredients to create a culinary masterpiece, a data scientist needs high-quality data to build effective models.

Types of Data

- **Numerical data:** Quantitative information expressed as numbers (e.g., age, temperature, salary).

Numerical data, often referred to as **quantitative data**, is information expressed as numbers. It is measurable, countable, and forms the foundation for statistical analysis and machine learning models.

Key Characteristics of Numerical Data:

- **Quantifiable:** Can be measured and expressed in numerical terms.
- **Ordered:** Values can be arranged in a specific order (ascending or descending).
- **Arithmetic operations:** Mathematical operations like addition, subtraction, multiplication, and division can be performed.

Types of Numerical Data:

- **Discrete Data:** Takes on specific, distinct values (e.g., number of children, count of items).
- **Continuous Data:** Can take on any value within a range (e.g., height, weight, temperature).

Examples of Numerical Data:

- Age
- Salary
- Temperature
- Product price

- **Number of customers**
- **Test scores**

Importance of Numerical Data in Machine Learning

Numerical data is essential for training most machine learning algorithms. Techniques like linear regression, decision trees, and neural networks heavily rely on numerical inputs to make predictions or classifications.

- **Categorical data:** Qualitative information representing categories or groups (e.g., gender, country, color).

Categorical data represents qualitative information that can be grouped into distinct categories or labels. Unlike numerical data, categorical data doesn't have inherent numerical value.

Key Characteristics of Categorical Data:

- **Qualitative:** Describes qualities or characteristics rather than quantities.
- **Unordered or Ordered:** Categorical data can be either nominal (no inherent order) or ordinal (has a specific order).
- **Non-numeric:** Values are represented by labels or text.

Types of Categorical Data:

- **Nominal Data:** Categories have no inherent order or ranking.
    - Examples: Gender, country, color, occupation.

- **Ordinal Data:** Categories have a natural order or ranking.
    - Examples: Education level (high school, bachelor's, master's), product rating (poor, good, excellent).

Handling Categorical Data in Machine Learning:

- **Encoding:** Converting categorical data into a numerical format for machine learning algorithms.
    - **One-hot encoding:** Creating binary columns for each category.
    - **Label encoding:** Assigning numerical labels to categories.
- **Feature engineering:** Creating new features based on categorical data.

By understanding the nuances of categorical data and applying appropriate encoding techniques, you can effectively incorporate it into your machine learning models.

- **Text data:** Unstructured information in textual format (e.g., product reviews, social media posts).

Text data is unstructured information presented in textual format. It's abundant in today's digital world, found in emails, social media posts, product reviews, articles, and more. While challenging to process due to its unstructured nature, it holds immense value for extracting insights and building intelligent applications.

Key Characteristics of Text Data:

- **Unstructured:** Lacks predefined data models or organization.
- **High dimensionality:** The vocabulary size can be vast.
- **Noise:** Contains irrelevant information, typos, and inconsistencies.
- **Contextual:** The meaning of words can vary based on context.

Challenges in Handling Text Data:

- **Preprocessing:** Cleaning, tokenization, and normalization are essential steps.
- **Feature extraction:** Converting text into numerical representations for machine learning algorithms.
- **Model selection:** Choosing appropriate algorithms for text-based tasks.
- **Evaluation:** Measuring model performance using relevant metrics.

Common Text Data Analysis Tasks:

- **Sentiment analysis:** Determining the sentiment expressed in text (positive, negative, neutral).
- **Text classification:** Categorizing text into predefined classes (spam/ham, news topics).
- **Topic modeling:** Discovering underlying themes or topics within a collection of documents.
- **Named entity recognition (NER):** Identifying and classifying named entities (persons, organizations, locations).
- **Text summarization:** Generating concise summaries of lengthy documents.

By mastering techniques for handling text data, you can unlock valuable insights and build intelligent applications.

- **Image data:** Visual information captured in digital format (e.g., photos, medical images).

Image data represents visual information captured in a digital format. It consists of pixels arranged in a grid, with each pixel containing color or intensity values. This data forms the foundation for computer vision tasks, enabling machines to interpret and understand visual content.

Key Characteristics of Image Data:

- **High dimensionality:** Images often contain a large number of pixels, leading to high-dimensional data.
- **Unstructured:** Unlike tabular data, images lack predefined formats or structures.
- **Spatial relationships:** The arrangement of pixels is crucial for understanding image content.

Common Image Formats:

- **JPEG:** Widely used for photographs due to its compression efficiency.
- **PNG:** Supports lossless compression, preserving image quality.
- **BMP:** Uncompressed format, often used for raw image data.
- **TIFF:** Versatile format for high-quality images, supporting various compression options.

Challenges in Handling Image Data:

- **Data volume:** Images can be large, requiring efficient storage and processing.
- **Noise and artifacts:** Images often contain imperfections that need to be addressed.
- **Feature extraction:** Converting images into numerical representations for machine learning.

Applications of Image Data:

- **Image classification:** Categorizing images into predefined classes (e.g., cat, dog, car).
- **Object detection:** Identifying and locating objects within an image.
- **Image segmentation:** Dividing an image into meaningful regions.
- **Image generation:** Creating new images or modifying existing ones.

By understanding the nature of image data and applying appropriate techniques, you can unlock valuable insights and build powerful computer vision applications.

Data Collection Techniques

- **Surveys and questionnaires:** Gathering data directly from individuals.

Surveys and questionnaires are powerful tools for gathering data directly from individuals. They provide valuable insights into opinions, behaviors, preferences, and demographics.

Key Characteristics of Survey Data:

- **Direct from the source:** Provides firsthand information from respondents.
- **Versatile:** Can collect both quantitative and qualitative data.
- **Subjective:** Responses can be influenced by personal biases and opinions.

Types of Surveys:

- **Online surveys:** Conducted through web-based platforms.
- **Mail surveys:** Distributed through postal mail.
- **Telephone surveys:** Conducted over the phone.
- **Face-to-face interviews:** In-person interactions with respondents.

Challenges in Survey Data:

- **Response rate:** Ensuring a sufficient number of completed surveys.
- **Data quality:** Addressing issues like missing data, inconsistent responses, and biases.
- **Survey design:** Crafting clear and unbiased questions.

Effective Survey Design:

- **Clear objectives:** Define the goals of the survey.
- **Target audience:** Identify the specific population to be surveyed.
- **Question types:** Use a mix of open-ended and closed-ended questions.
- **Length:** Keep surveys concise to maintain respondent engagement.
- **Incentives:** Consider offering incentives to increase response rates.

By carefully designing and conducting surveys, you can collect valuable data to inform decision-making and gain insights into your target audience.

- **Web scraping:** Extracting data from websites.

Web scraping is the process of extracting data from websites. It involves automating the process of fetching, parsing, and extracting information from web pages. This data can then be used for various purposes, such as market research, data analysis, and machine learning.

Key Components of Web Scraping:

- **HTML Parsing:** Understanding the structure of web pages to identify data elements.
- **Data Extraction:** Isolating specific information from the HTML code.
- **Data Cleaning:** Preparing the extracted data for analysis.
- **Storage:** Saving the extracted data in a suitable format (CSV, JSON, database).

Challenges in Web Scraping:

- **Dynamic content:** Websites that load data using JavaScript can be challenging.
- **Website changes:** Websites often update their structure, requiring script modifications.
- **Legal and ethical considerations:** Respecting website terms of service and avoiding copyright infringement.
- **Rate limiting:** Adhering to website restrictions on data retrieval.

Tools and Libraries:

- **Beautiful Soup:** A Python library for parsing HTML and XML documents.
- **Scrapy:** A Python framework for large-scale web scraping projects.
- **Selenium:** For handling dynamic websites and interacting with web elements.
- **Requests:** For making HTTP requests to fetch web pages.

By mastering web scraping techniques, you can access a vast amount of data that would otherwise be inaccessible. However, it's essential to use these tools responsibly and ethically.

- **APIs:** Accessing data from external sources through programming interfaces.

APIs (Application Programming Interfaces) are essentially messengers that allow different software applications to communicate and interact with each other. They provide a defined set of rules and protocols for accessing and manipulating data.

Key Characteristics of APIs:

- **Standardized interface:** A consistent way to interact with a system or service.
- **Data exchange:** Facilitates the transfer of data between applications.
- **Efficiency:** Streamlines data access and reduces development time.
- **Security:** Often includes authentication and authorization mechanisms.

Types of APIs:

- **Open APIs:** Publicly accessible APIs, often used for integrating third-party services.
- **Partner APIs:** Shared between collaborating organizations.
- **Internal APIs:** Used within an organization to connect different systems.
- **Composite APIs:** Combine multiple APIs to provide a unified interface.

Common API Protocols:

- **REST (Representational State Transfer):** Most common, using HTTP methods (GET, POST, PUT, DELETE).
- **SOAP (Simple Object Access Protocol):** XML-based protocol for structured data exchange.
- **GraphQL:** Flexible API for fetching specific data.

Benefits of Using APIs:

- **Data enrichment:** Combine data from multiple sources.
- **Automation:** Integrate with external services for automated tasks.
- **Innovation:** Build new applications and services based on existing data.

By effectively utilizing APIs, you can tap into a vast amount of data and create powerful applications.

- **Databases:** Retrieving data from structured repositories.

Databases are structured repositories designed to store, manage, and retrieve large volumes of data efficiently. They provide a foundation for various applications, including business intelligence, data analysis, and machine learning.

Key Components of a Database:

- **Tables:** Organized collections of data with rows (records) and columns (fields).
- **Records:** Individual instances of data within a table.
- **Fields:** Specific pieces of information within a record.
- **Indexes:** Structures that speed up data retrieval.
- **Relationships:** Connections between tables (one-to-one, one-to-many, many-to-many).

Types of Databases:

- **Relational Databases:** Store data in tables with relationships between them (e.g., MySQL, PostgreSQL, SQL Server).
- **NoSQL Databases:** Handle unstructured or semi-structured data (e.g., MongoDB, Cassandra).
- **Data Warehouses:** Store and manage large volumes of data for analysis and reporting.
- **Data Lakes:** Store raw data in its native format for exploratory analysis.

SQL: The Language of Databases

SQL (Structured Query Language) is the standard language for interacting with relational databases. It allows you to:

- **Retrieve data:** Select specific data based on various criteria.
- **Insert data:** Add new records to a table.
- **Update data:** Modify existing data within a table.
- **Delete data:** Remove records from a table.

- **Sensors:** Collecting data from physical devices.

Sensors are devices that detect and respond to physical stimuli. They convert real-world phenomena into electrical signals that can be processed by computers. This data collection process is fundamental to various applications, from industrial automation to consumer electronics.

Types of Sensors:

- **Temperature sensors:** Measure temperature (e.g., thermocouples, thermistors).
- **Pressure sensors:** Detect pressure changes (e.g., barometers, strain gauges).

- **Motion sensors:** Detect movement (e.g., accelerometers, gyroscopes).
- **Light sensors:** Measure light intensity (e.g., photodiodes, photoresistors).
- **Proximity sensors:** Detect objects within a specific distance (e.g., ultrasonic, infrared).
- **Environmental sensors:** Monitor environmental conditions (e.g., humidity, air quality).

Applications of Sensor Data:

- **IoT (Internet of Things):** Connecting physical devices to the internet for data collection and remote monitoring.
- **Industrial automation:** Optimizing production processes and quality control.
- **Healthcare:** Monitoring patient vitals, wearable devices.
- **Automotive:** Advanced driver assistance systems (ADAS), autonomous vehicles.
- **Smart homes:** Energy management, security systems, home automation.

Challenges in Sensor Data:

- **Noise:** Dealing with unwanted signals or interference.
- **Data volume:** Managing large amounts of data generated by sensors.
- **Data quality:** Ensuring data accuracy and reliability.
- **Data integration:** Combining sensor data with other data sources.

By understanding the types of sensors, their capabilities, and the challenges involved, you can effectively harness the power of sensor data for various applications.

The Importance of Data Quality

High-quality data is essential for building accurate and reliable models. Key factors include:

- **Accuracy:** Data should be correct and free from errors.

Accuracy is a fundamental aspect of data quality. It ensures that data correctly reflects the real-world entities it represents. Inaccurate data can lead to erroneous conclusions, poor decision-making, and financial losses.

Key Components of Data Accuracy:

- **Correctness:** Data values match the true values of the attributes they represent.
- **Precision:** Data is specific and detailed enough to meet the intended purpose.
- **Reliability:** Data can be consistently trusted to be accurate.

Ensuring Data Accuracy:

- **Data validation:** Implementing checks to verify data integrity during input.
- **Data cleaning:** Identifying and correcting errors, inconsistencies, and outliers.
- **Data verification:** Comparing data against trusted sources or reference data.

- **Data standardization:** Establishing consistent data formats and definitions.

Impact of Inaccurate Data:

- **Biased models:** Inaccurate data can lead to biased machine learning models.
- **Incorrect decisions:** Erroneous conclusions based on faulty data.
- **Financial losses:** Inaccurate data can result in financial penalties or lost opportunities.
- **Reputation damage:** Errors in public-facing data can harm an organization's credibility.

By prioritizing data accuracy, organizations can build trust, improve decision-making, and enhance the overall value of their data assets.

- **Completeness:** Data should have minimal missing values.

Data completeness refers to the extent to which a dataset contains all necessary information. Missing values can significantly impact data analysis and model performance.

Importance of Data Completeness:

- **Accurate analysis:** Missing data can skew results and lead to incorrect conclusions.
- **Model performance:** Incomplete data can reduce the accuracy of machine learning models.
- **Decision making:** Missing information can hinder effective decision-making.

Handling Missing Data:

- **Deletion:** Removing records with missing values (can lead to data loss).
- **Imputation:** Filling missing values with estimated values:
    - Mean/median/mode imputation
    - K-Nearest Neighbors (KNN) imputation
    - Multiple imputation
    - Predictive models
- **Analysis with missing data:** Employing techniques designed for datasets with missing values.

By addressing missing data effectively, you can improve the quality and reliability of your data, leading to better insights and model performance.

- **Consistency:** Data should be formatted uniformly.

Data consistency ensures that data is formatted and structured uniformly across a dataset. It's essential for accurate analysis and reliable insights.

Importance of Data Consistency:

- **Data integration:** Consistent data formats facilitate seamless integration from multiple sources.
- **Data analysis:** Uniform data enables accurate calculations and comparisons.
- **Data quality:** Consistent data reduces errors and improves data reliability.

- **Model performance:** Inconsistent data can negatively impact machine learning model accuracy.

Achieving Data Consistency:

- **Standardization:** Define and enforce consistent data formats, units, and codes.
- **Data cleaning:** Identify and correct inconsistencies, errors, and outliers.
- **Data validation:** Implement checks to ensure data adheres to defined standards.
- **Metadata management:** Document data definitions, formats, and sources.

Examples of Data Inconsistencies:

- **Different date formats:** DD/MM/YYYY, MM/DD/YYYY.
- **Inconsistent currency symbols:** $, €, ¥.
- **Varying units of measurement:** meters, feet, kilometers.
- **Spelling errors:** Different spellings for the same entity.

By maintaining data consistency, you can significantly enhance the quality and value of your data, leading to more accurate and reliable insights.

- **Relevance:** Data should be relevant to the problem you're trying to solve.

Data relevance signifies the degree to which data is pertinent to the specific problem or question being addressed. It's crucial to ensure that the data collected and analyzed directly contributes to the desired outcome.

Importance of Data Relevance:

- **Accurate insights:** Relevant data provides accurate and meaningful information.
- **Efficient analysis:** Reduces time spent on irrelevant data processing.
- **Cost-effective:** Avoids unnecessary data collection and storage.
- **Improved decision-making:** Supports informed choices based on pertinent information.

Ensuring Data Relevance:

- **Clear problem definition:** Clearly articulate the problem to identify necessary data.
- **Data selection:** Focus on collecting and using data directly related to the problem.
- **Data cleaning:** Remove irrelevant or redundant data.
- **Feature engineering:** Create relevant features from raw data.

By prioritizing data relevance, organizations can optimize their data resources and derive maximum value from their analytics initiatives.

By mastering data collection, cleaning, and preparation, you'll set the stage for building powerful machine learning models.

- **Algorithms: The Recipe for Success:** Just as a recipe guides a chef in creating a dish, algorithms provide the instructions for ML models. This chapter will introduce you to different types of algorithms, such as linear regression for prediction or decision trees for classification. We'll break down the core concepts of these algorithms in an understandable way, without getting bogged down in complex mathematical details.

Algorithms are the heart and soul of machine learning. They provide the step-by-step instructions for a model to learn from data and make predictions or decisions.

Understanding Different Types of Algorithms

- **Supervised Learning:** Algorithms learn from labeled data.
    - **Linear Regression:** Predicts a continuous numerical value (e.g., house prices).
    - **Logistic Regression:** Predicts a categorical outcome (e.g., spam or not spam).
    - **Decision Trees:** Creates a tree-like model of decisions and their possible consequences.
    - **Random Forest:** Combines multiple decision trees to improve accuracy.
    - **Support Vector Machines (SVMs):** Finds the best hyperplane to separate data points.
- **Unsupervised Learning:** Algorithms find patterns in unlabeled data.
    - **Clustering:** Groups similar data points together (e.g., customer segmentation).
    - **Dimensionality Reduction:** Reduces the number of features while preserving information.

We'll explore these and other algorithms in detail, focusing on their core concepts and how they work without diving too deep into the math.

The Marriage of Data and Algorithms: The magic happens when data and algorithms come together. We'll explore how data is prepared and fed into the chosen algorithm. You'll understand how the algorithm learns from the data, identifies patterns, and makes predictions based on those patterns.

The synergy between data and algorithms is the cornerstone of machine learning. Let's break down this magical process:

Preparing Data for the Algorithm

- **Data Cleaning:** Handling missing values, outliers, and inconsistencies.

Data cleaning is a critical step in the data preprocessing pipeline. It involves handling missing values, outliers, and inconsistencies to ensure data quality and reliability.

Handling Missing Values

Missing values can significantly impact data analysis. Here are common approaches:

- **Deletion:** Removing rows or columns with missing values.
- **Imputation:** Replacing missing values with estimated values:
    - Mean/median/mode imputation
    - K-Nearest Neighbors (KNN) imputation
    - Multiple imputation
    - Predictive models

Handling Outliers

Outliers are data points that deviate significantly from other observations. They can be caused by errors, anomalies, or true extremes.

- **Detection:** Use statistical methods like z-scores, box plots, or interquartile range.
- **Treatment:** Remove, cap, or transform outliers based on their impact and domain knowledge.

Handling Inconsistencies

Inconsistencies in data can lead to erroneous results.

- **Standardization:** Ensure consistent formatting for dates, numbers, and text.
- **Data validation:** Verify data against predefined rules and constraints.
- **Error correction:** Correct inaccurate or conflicting data.

Additional Considerations

- **Domain knowledge:** Understanding the data context is crucial for effective cleaning.
- **Iterative process:** Data cleaning often involves multiple iterations.
- **Tool selection:** Utilize appropriate libraries and tools for efficient cleaning (e.g., Pandas, NumPy).

By carefully addressing missing values, outliers, and inconsistencies, you can improve the quality and reliability of your data, leading to more accurate and meaningful insights.

- **Feature Engineering:** Creating new features or transforming existing ones to improve model performance.

Feature engineering is the process of transforming raw data into features that are suitable for machine learning algorithms. It involves selecting, extracting, and transforming relevant information from the data to enhance model performance.

Key Techniques in Feature Engineering:

- **Feature creation:** Combining existing features to generate new ones.
  - Examples: Creating interaction terms, polynomial features, or ratio features.
- **Feature transformation:** Modifying existing features to improve their distribution or scale.
  - Examples: Normalization, standardization, log transformation.
- **Feature scaling:** Adjusting the range of features to a common scale.
  - Examples: Min-max scaling, z-score normalization.
- **Feature selection:** Identifying and retaining the most relevant features for the model.
  - Examples: Correlation analysis, feature importance, recursive feature elimination.

Importance of Feature Engineering:

- **Improved model performance:** Well-engineered features can significantly boost model accuracy and generalization.
- **Enhanced interpretability:** Meaningful features make models easier to understand.
- **Reduced dimensionality:** Simplifying the data can speed up training and improve efficiency.

By carefully crafting features, you can unlock the hidden potential of your data and build more effective machine learning models.

- **Data Splitting:** Dividing data into training, validation, and test sets.

Data splitting is a crucial step in the machine learning process. It involves dividing the dataset into three distinct subsets:

- **Training set:** Used to train the model, learning patterns from the data.
- **Validation set:** Used to tune hyperparameters and evaluate model performance during training.
- **Test set:** Used to assess the final model's performance on unseen data.

Why Split the Data?

- **Preventing overfitting:** Overfitting occurs when a model learns the training data too well, performing poorly on new data.
- **Hyperparameter tuning:** The validation set helps select the best model configuration.

- **Unbiased evaluation:** The test set provides an unbiased estimate of the model's generalization ability.

Common Split Ratios:

- **70/15/15:** 70% training, 15% validation, 15% testing.
- **80/10/10:** 80% training, 10% validation, 10% testing.

Techniques for Data Splitting:

- **Random splitting:** Randomly dividing the data into subsets.
- **Stratified sampling:** Ensuring representative samples of each class in the dataset.
- **Time-based splitting:** Used for time-series data to preserve temporal order.

By carefully dividing your data into training, validation, and test sets, you can build robust and reliable machine learning models.

- **Data Scaling:** Normalizing or standardizing numerical features.

Data scaling is a crucial preprocessing step in machine learning to ensure that features are on a comparable scale. It prevents features with larger values from dominating the learning process.

Normalization

- **Scales features to a specific range**, typically between 0 and 1.

- Useful when features have different ranges and the distribution is not important.
- Formula: (x - min(x)) / (max(x) - min(x))

Standardization

- **Scales features to have a mean of 0 and a standard deviation of 1.**
- Assumes data follows a normal distribution.
- Often preferred for algorithms sensitive to feature scale (e.g., SVM, logistic regression).
- Formula: (x - mean(x)) / std(x)

When to Use Which

- **Normalization:** When the data distribution is not Gaussian and the feature range matters (e.g., image pixel values).
- **Standardization:** When the data is normally distributed or when the feature range doesn't matter (e.g., most statistical models).

Importance of Data Scaling

- **Improves model performance:** Many algorithms are sensitive to feature scales.
- **Faster convergence:** Scaled features can accelerate training.
- **Better interpretation:** Scaled features can sometimes enhance interpretability.

By applying appropriate scaling techniques, you can significantly improve the performance of your machine learning models.

Feeding Data to the Algorithm

- **Training Phase:** The algorithm learns patterns from the training data.
- **Model Building:** The algorithm creates a mathematical representation of the underlying patterns.
- **Optimization:** Adjusting model parameters to minimize errors.

Algorithm Learning and Prediction

- **Pattern Recognition:** The algorithm identifies relationships between features and the target variable.
- **Model Evaluation:** Assessing the model's performance on the validation set.
- **Prediction:** Using the trained model to make predictions on new, unseen data.

By understanding this process, you'll be well-equipped to build effective machine learning models.

CHAPTER FOUR

Supervised learning and unsupervised learning

In the world of machine learning (ML), not all problems are created equal. Just like choosing the right tool for the job, selecting the appropriate learning approach is crucial for success. This chapter explores the two main categories of ML: supervised learning and unsupervised learning.

Supervised Learning:

Imagine a student learning with a helpful teacher who provides labeled examples. Supervised learning operates in a similar way. It involves training models using labeled data, where each data point has a corresponding output value or label. The model learns the relationship between the input data and the desired output, allowing it to make predictions for new, unseen data.

Supervised learning is indeed like having a knowledgeable teacher guiding the learning process. By providing labeled data, we're essentially providing a set of correct answers for the model to learn from.

Key Components of Supervised Learning:

- **Labeled Dataset:** Contains input data (features) and corresponding output labels (targets).

- **Model Selection:** Choosing the appropriate algorithm based on the problem type (classification or regression).
- **Training:** The model learns patterns from the labeled data to map inputs to outputs.
- **Evaluation:** Assessing the model's performance on a separate test dataset.
- **Prediction:** Using the trained model to make predictions on new, unseen data.

Applications of Supervised Learning:

- Spam filtering: Classifies emails as spam or not spam based on labeled examples.
- Image recognition: Identifies objects in images after being trained on labeled images.
- Stock price prediction: Predicts future stock prices based on historical labeled data.

Let's break down how supervised learning is applied in each case:

Spam Filtering

- **Labeled data:** Emails labeled as spam or not spam.
- **Algorithm:** Typically, a Naive Bayes classifier or Support Vector Machine (SVM) is used.
- **Learning:** The algorithm learns to identify patterns in spam emails, such as specific words, phrases, or sender information.
- **Prediction:** When a new email arrives, the model classifies it as spam or not spam based on the learned patterns.

Image Recognition

- **Labeled data:** Images with corresponding labels (e.g., cat, dog, car).
- **Algorithm:** Convolutional Neural Networks (CNNs) are commonly used for image recognition.
- **Learning:** The model learns to extract features from images and associate them with specific labels.
- **Prediction:** When presented with a new image, the model identifies the objects or scenes within it.

Stock Price Prediction

- **Labeled data:** Historical stock prices with corresponding dates.
- **Algorithm:** Regression algorithms like Linear Regression or more complex models like Recurrent Neural Networks (RNNs) can be used.
- **Learning:** The model identifies patterns in historical stock prices to understand trends and fluctuations.
- **Prediction:** The model forecasts future stock prices based on the learned patterns.

Unsupervised Learning:

Now imagine a student exploring a new subject without any specific guidance. Unsupervised learning works in a similar way. It involves analyzing unlabeled data, where the data points lack predefined categories or labels. The goal is to uncover hidden patterns or structures within the data itself.

Unsupervised learning is like exploring a new city without a map. You rely on your observations to discover hidden gems, neighborhoods, and potential connections.

Key Components of Unsupervised Learning

- **Unlabeled Data:** Data without predefined categories or labels.
- **Pattern Discovery:** Identifying underlying structures or relationships within the data.
- **Clustering:** Grouping similar data points together based on their features.
- **Dimensionality Reduction:** Simplifying data by reducing the number of features while preserving essential information.

Common Unsupervised Learning Algorithms

- **K-means Clustering:** Partitions data into K clusters.
- **Hierarchical Clustering:** Creates a hierarchy of clusters.
- **Principal Component Analysis (PCA):** Reduces dimensionality while retaining variance.

  Applications of Unsupervised Learning:

  - Customer segmentation: Groups customers with similar characteristics based on their purchase history (unlabeled data).
  - Anomaly detection: Identifies unusual patterns in data, like fraudulent credit card transactions.
  - Recommendation systems: Recommends products to users based on their past behavior and similar user preferences (unlabeled data).

Examples of unsupervised learning applications

Customer Segmentation

- **Unlabeled data:** Customer purchase history, demographics, and behavior.
- **Goal:** Identify distinct customer groups with similar characteristics.
- **Algorithm:** K-means clustering or hierarchical clustering is often used.
- **Benefits:** Tailored marketing campaigns, product recommendations, and improved customer satisfaction.

Anomaly Detection

- **Unlabeled data:** Historical data of normal behavior (e.g., credit card transactions, network traffic).
- **Goal:** Identify unusual patterns that deviate from normal behavior.
- **Algorithm:** Isolation Forest, One-Class SVM, or Autoencoders can be used.
- **Benefits:** Fraud prevention, system monitoring, and quality control.

Recommendation Systems

- **Unlabeled data:** User behavior, product information, and ratings (if available).
- **Goal:** Suggest relevant items to users based on their preferences and similarities to other users.
- **Algorithm:** Collaborative filtering, content-based filtering, or hybrid approaches can be employed.
- **Benefits:** Increased sales, improved customer engagement, and personalized experiences.

CHAPTER FIVE

Training, validation, and testing

Imagine you're training a dog to fetch. You wouldn't just throw the ball once and expect it to understand. In machine learning (ML), the learning process is similar – it involves a carefully structured journey for your model. This chapter delves into the three crucial stages: training, validation, and testing.

Training:

This is where the magic happens! During training, your ML model is exposed to a large portion of your data. Each data point acts as a training example, helping the model learn the underlying patterns and relationships within the data. Think of it like your dog learning to associate the act of fetching with getting a treat (positive reinforcement).

Training is indeed the cornerstone of machine learning. It's where the model learns to recognize patterns and make informed decisions.

Key aspects of training:

- **Data Preparation:** Ensuring data is clean, formatted correctly, and divided into training and validation sets.
- **Model Selection:** Choosing the appropriate algorithm based on the problem type.

- **Iterative Process:** The model is repeatedly exposed to the training data, adjusting its parameters with each iteration.
- **Loss Function:** A metric used to measure the model's performance and guide the learning process.
- **Optimization:** Adjusting model parameters to minimize the loss function.

The Role of Algorithms:

The chosen algorithm acts as the training guide, defining how the model learns from the data. Different algorithms have different learning approaches, but all aim to minimize errors in the model's predictions.

Algorithms are the architects of machine learning models. They define the blueprint for how the model learns from data.

Key roles of algorithms:

- **Learning Process:** Dictates how the model extracts patterns from data.
- **Model Complexity:** Determines the model's capacity to capture intricate relationships.
- **Performance:** Impacts the model's accuracy, speed, and resource utilization.

By understanding different algorithms and their strengths, you can select the best tool for the job.

Metrics for Success:

We need to measure how well our model is learning. Here, we introduce performance metrics like accuracy or error rate. These metrics tell us how closely the model's predictions align with the actual values in the training data.

Key Performance Metrics:

- **Accuracy:** The proportion of correct predictions to total predictions (suitable for balanced datasets).
- **Precision:** The ratio of correct positive predictions to total positive predictions (useful when false positives are costly).
- **Recall:** The ratio of correct positive predictions to actual positive cases (important when false negatives are costly).
- **F1-score:** The harmonic mean of precision and recall, providing a balance between the two.
- **Mean Squared Error (MSE):** Measures the average squared difference between predicted and actual values (for regression problems).

Choosing the Right Metric:

The choice of metric depends on the specific problem and desired outcome. For example:

- **Spam filtering:** Precision and recall are crucial to minimize false positives and false negatives.
- **Image recognition:** Accuracy might be sufficient if classes are balanced.
- **Stock price prediction:** MSE or Mean Absolute Error (MAE) can be used to evaluate prediction accuracy.

Validation:

Imagine a dog that only fetches a specific type of ball – it's overfit to that particular experience. In ML, overfitting occurs when the model memorizes the training data too well, leading to poor performance on unseen data.

Validation helps prevent this. A smaller portion of your data, separate from the training set, is used for validation. The model is evaluated on this data to identify signs of overfitting. If the model performs poorly on the validation set, it might be a sign that it's overfitting the training data.

Validation is indeed a crucial step in preventing overfitting. It acts as a safety net, ensuring our model can generalize well to unseen data.

Key points about validation:

- **Early Stopping:** This technique involves monitoring the performance on the validation set during training and stopping the training process when performance starts to degrade.
- **Cross-Validation:** A more robust method where the data is divided into multiple folds, and the model is trained and evaluated on different combinations of folds.

By incorporating validation into the machine learning pipeline, we can build more reliable and robust models.

Testing:

Once you're confident your model has learned effectively, it's time for the final test. A completely separate data set, unseen by the model during training or validation, is used for testing. This provides a realistic assessment of how well the model generalizes and performs on new data.

Testing is the ultimate crucible for a machine learning model.

Key points about testing:

- **Independence:** The test set should be entirely separate from the training and validation sets.
- **Real-world Evaluation:** It provides a realistic assessment of the model's performance in a new environment.
- **Model Selection:** Comparing test set performance of different models helps in selecting the best one.
- **Iterative Process:** If the model underperforms on the test set, it might necessitate revisiting data preparation, feature

engineering, or algorithm selection.

By rigorously testing our models, we can ensure they are ready for real-world deployment.

The Importance of All Three Stages:

Training, validation, and testing are all crucial for building robust and reliable ML models. By following this structured learning process, you ensure your model doesn't just memorize the training data, but can effectively learn and apply its knowledge to unseen situations.

The synergy between training, validation, and testing is essential for building robust and reliable machine learning models. By following this structured approach, we ensure that our models can generalize well to new, unseen data.

Key benefits of this process:

- **Prevents overfitting:** Validation helps identify and mitigate overfitting issues.

Validation is a crucial step in mitigating overfitting. Let's explore some techniques in more detail:

Techniques to Prevent Overfitting

- **Regularization:**
    - L1 and L2 regularization: Penalize large model coefficients, encouraging simpler models.
    - Dropout: Randomly deactivates neurons during training, preventing overreliance on specific features.

- **Data Augmentation:** Increasing the size and diversity of the training data by creating modified versions of existing data.
- **Early Stopping:** Halting the training process when performance on the validation set starts to deteriorate.
- **Feature Selection:** Choosing the most relevant features to reduce model complexity.
- **Ensemble Methods:** Combining multiple models to improve generalization.

- **Improves model performance:** Iterative refinement based on validation results leads to better models.

Iterative Refinement:

The iterative process of refining a model based on validation results is crucial for achieving optimal performance. It's akin to a scientist conducting experiments and adjusting their hypothesis based on the findings.

Key aspects of iterative refinement:

- **Hyperparameter Tuning:** Optimizing hyperparameters like learning rate, batch size, and regularization strength to improve model performance.
- **Feature Engineering:** Creating new features or transforming existing ones to better capture underlying patterns.
- **Algorithm Selection:** Experimenting with different algorithms to find the best fit for the problem.
- **Data Exploration:** Further investigating the data for potential insights and improvements.

By continuously refining the model based on validation feedback, we can significantly enhance its predictive power.

- **Enhances model reliability:** Testing provides a final, unbiased assessment of model performance.

Testing:

Testing is the ultimate crucible for a machine learning model. It's the final checkpoint to ensure the model's readiness for real-world applications.

Key aspects of testing:

- **Unbiased Evaluation:** The test set provides an unbiased assessment of the model's performance on unseen data.
- **Model Selection:** Comparing the performance of multiple models on the test set helps in selecting the best candidate.
- **Deployment Readiness:** A strong performance on the test set indicates the model is ready for deployment.
- **Error Analysis:** Identifying patterns in errors can provide valuable insights for model improvement.

CHAPTER SIX

Choosing a Programming Language

Machine learning (ML) is a powerful field, but it requires the right tools to bring your ideas to life. One of the most important choices you'll make is selecting a programming language. This chapter will explore popular options and help you pick the best fit for your learning journey.

Top contenders in the ML language arena:

- **Python:** Often crowned the king of ML languages, Python is known for its:
    - **Readability:** Its clear and concise syntax makes it easy to learn and understand, even for beginners.
    - **Extensive Libraries:** A rich ecosystem of libraries like TensorFlow, PyTorch, and scikit-learn provide pre-built tools and functionalities for various ML tasks.
    - **Large Community:** A vast and active community offers abundant resources, tutorials, and support for Python-based ML projects.

Python: The Unsurpassed Champion for Machine Learning

You've spotlighted Python's key strengths for machine learning perfectly!

Its combination of readability, extensive libraries, and a vast community has solidified its position as the go-to language for data scientists and machine learning engineers.

Let's add a few more points to highlight Python's dominance:

- **Versatility:** Beyond machine learning, Python is used in web development, data analysis, scientific computing, and more, making it a valuable skill for a wide range of roles.
- **Rapid Prototyping:** Python's interactive nature and ease of use allow for quick experimentation and iteration in the model development process.
- **Integration Capabilities:** Python seamlessly integrates with other languages and tools, enabling the creation of complex ML pipelines.

- **R:** A popular choice among statisticians and data analysts, R offers:
    - **Statistical Strength:** Built-in statistical functions and packages cater specifically to data analysis and exploration, making it ideal for tasks heavily reliant on statistics.
    - **Data Visualization:** R excels in creating informative and visually appealing data visualizations.

R: The Statistician's Choice

You've accurately highlighted R's strengths. It's indeed a powerful tool for statisticians and data analysts.

Let's add a few more points:

- **Open-Source Community:** R benefits from a large and active community contributing to its development and providing extensive support.
- **Specialized Packages:** A vast ecosystem of packages caters to specific domains like finance, bioinformatics, and social sciences.

R's emphasis on statistical modeling and data visualization makes it an excellent choice for tasks requiring deep statistical analysis.

- **Java:** A robust and mature language, Java provides:
    - **Scalability and Performance:** Ideal for large-scale, enterprise-level ML projects requiring high performance and scalability.
    - **Object-Oriented Design:** Java's object-oriented structure promotes code reusability and modularity, beneficial for complex projects.

Java: The Robust Workhorse for Machine Learning

Java's strengths in scalability and performance make it an ideal choice for large-scale, enterprise-level machine learning projects.

Let's add a few more points:

- **Mature Ecosystem:** Java boasts a rich ecosystem of libraries and frameworks, such as Weka, Deeplearning4j, and H2O, supporting various ML tasks.
- **Enterprise Adoption:** Java's widespread use in enterprise environments makes it a natural choice for integrating ML solutions into existing systems.

- **Strong Type System:** While this might seem restrictive for rapid prototyping, it ensures code reliability and maintainability in large-scale projects.

- Hands-on Example: Building a Simple Model (e.g., Linear Regression)

Hands-on Example:

Welcome to the exciting world of hands-on machine learning (ML)! This chapter will guide you through building your first model using a popular technique called linear regression.

Linear Regression:

Imagine predicting house prices based on their size. Linear regression excels at this kind of task. It creates a best-fit line that captures the relationship between a single continuous variable (like house size) and a continuous target variable (like house price).

Building our Model: Step-by-Step

We'll use Python and a popular library called scikit-learn to build our model. Don't worry if you're new to Python; we'll break it down step-by-step.

1. **Import Necessary Libraries:**

We'll start by importing libraries like pandas (for data manipulation) and scikit-learn (for building the model).

1. **Load and Explore Data:**

Imagine we have a dataset containing house size and price information. We'll use pandas to read this data into a DataFrame and explore it to understand its characteristics.

3. **Data Preparation:**

Our data might need some cleaning and preparation before feeding it to the model. This could involve handling missing values, converting data types, or creating new features.

4. **Splitting Data for Training and Testing:**

Remember the crucial stages of training, validation, and testing? Here, we'll split our data into two sets: a training set used to train the model and a testing set used to evaluate its performance on unseen data.

5. **Creating an Training the Model:**

Now comes the exciting part! We'll create a linear regression model using scikit-learn and train it on our training data.

6. **Making Predictions:**

The trained model can now predict prices for new house sizes (data it hasn't seen before) in the testing set.

7. **Evaluating Model Performance:**

We don't just trust the model blindly; we need to evaluate its performance. Here, we'll use metrics like mean squared error (MSE) to assess how well the predicted prices align with the actual prices in the testing set.

Debugging and Troubleshooting:

Debugging and troubleshooting are essential skills for any programmer or system administrator. While the terms are often used interchangeably, debugging typically focuses on code-level issues, while troubleshooting involves broader system problems.

Common Error Types and Troubleshooting Steps

Syntax Errors

- **Description:** Errors in the structure of the code, such as missing semicolons, mismatched parentheses, or incorrect keywords.
- **Common Causes:** Typos, incorrect indentation, missing punctuation.
- **Troubleshooting:**
    - Carefully review the code line by line.
    - Pay attention to error messages provided by the compiler or interpreter.
    - Use code formatting tools to improve readability.

Runtime Errors

- **Description:** Errors that occur during program execution, such as division by zero, accessing an out-of-bounds array index, or attempting to open a non-existent file.
- **Common Causes:** Logic errors, incorrect data, resource limitations.
- **Troubleshooting:**
    - Use debugging tools to step through the code and inspect variables.
    - Add print statements to track program flow and variable values.
    - Consider edge cases and input validation.

Logic Errors

- **Description:** Errors in the program's logic that produce incorrect results without causing the program to crash.
- **Common Causes:** Incorrect algorithms, faulty assumptions, missing code paths.
- **Troubleshooting:**
    - Carefully examine the program's logic and expected output.
    - Use test cases to verify program behavior.
    - Consider alternative approaches or algorithms.

Type Errors

- **Description:** Errors that occur due to incompatible data types, such as trying to add a string to an integer.
- **Common Causes:** Incorrect data types, type conversions, function arguments.
- **Troubleshooting:**
    - Check data types of variables and function parameters.
    - Use type conversion functions when necessary.
    - Consider using static typing or type hints to prevent these errors.

Resource Errors

- **Description:** Errors related to resource management, such as memory leaks, file access issues, or network connection problems.
- **Common Causes:** Improper resource allocation, failure to release resources, network issues.
- **Troubleshooting:**
    - Use memory profiling tools to identify memory leaks.
    - Check file permissions and paths.

- Verify network connectivity and troubleshoot network issues.

Debugging Techniques

- **Print Statements:** Insert print statements to track variable values and program flow.
- **Debugging Tools:** Use built-in debuggers or third-party tools to step through code, inspect variables, and set breakpoints.
- **Logging:** Record program events and errors in log files for later analysis.
- **Unit Testing:** Write tests to verify the correctness of individual code units.
- **Rubber Duck Debugging:** Explain the problem to someone or something (like a rubber duck) to clarify your thinking.

General Troubleshooting Tips

- **Reproduce the Error:** Consistently recreate the error to isolate the problem.
- **Isolate the Problem:** Break down the issue into smaller, manageable parts.
- **Search for Similar Issues:** Check online forums, documentation, or knowledge bases for solutions.
- **Test Changes Thoroughly:** Verify that any modifications fix the problem without introducing new issues.
- **Learn from Mistakes:** Document the error and its solution for future reference.

Additional Considerations

- **Programming Language Specific Errors:** Some languages have unique error types and handling mechanisms.
- **Framework or Library Issues:** Errors can arise from using third-party libraries or frameworks incorrectly.
- **Environment-Related Problems:** Issues can be caused by operating system configurations, hardware limitations, or network conditions.

CHAPTER SEVEN

What is Deep Learning

Deep learning is a subset of machine learning that utilizes artificial neural networks to learn complex patterns from large amounts of data. Inspired by the human brain, these networks consist of interconnected layers of nodes, allowing them to process information in a hierarchical manner.

How Does it Work?

1. **Data Preparation:** Data is collected, cleaned, and preprocessed to fit the neural network's requirements.
2. **Network Architecture:** A suitable neural network architecture is chosen based on the problem (e.g., convolutional neural networks for image recognition, recurrent neural networks for sequential data).
3. **Training:** The network learns from the data through a process called backpropagation, adjusting weights and biases to minimize error.
4. **Prediction:** Once trained, the network can make predictions or classifications on new, unseen data.

Key Components of a Neural Network

- **Neurons:** The basic units of a neural network, processing input and producing output.
- **Layers:** Groups of neurons organized into layers, including input, hidden, and output layers.
- **Weights and Biases:** Parameters that determine the strength of connections between neurons.
- **Activation Functions:** Introduce non-linearity, enabling the network to learn complex patterns.
- **Loss Function:** Measures the error between the network's output and the desired output.
- **Optimizer:** Adjusts weights and biases to minimize the loss function.

Types of Neural Networks

- **Convolutional Neural Networks (CNNs):** Excel at image and video analysis.

Convolutional Neural Networks (CNNs) are a specialized type of deep learning architecture designed to excel at image and video analysis tasks. They have revolutionized computer vision, enabling machines to understand and interpret visual data with remarkable accuracy.

Key Components of CNNs:

- **Convolutional layers:** Extract features from images by applying filters to detect patterns.
- **Pooling layers:** Reduce dimensionality and computational complexity while preserving important information.
- **Fully connected layers:** Combine features extracted from previous layers to make predictions.

How CNNs Work:

1. **Input:** An image is fed into the CNN as a numerical array.
2. **Convolutional layers:** Filters are applied to the image to extract features like edges, corners, and textures.
3. **Pooling layers:**Downsample the feature maps to reduce computational cost and improve invariance to small translations.
4. **Flattening:** Converts the output of the convolutional layers into a one-dimensional vector.
5. **Fully connected layers:** Process the flattened features and make predictions.

Applications of CNNs:

- **Image classification:** Categorizing images into different classes (e.g., cats vs. dogs).
- **Object detection:** Identifying and locating objects within an image.
- **Image segmentation:** Pixel-level classification of image regions.
- **Image generation:** Creating new images or modifying existing ones.
- **Video analysis:** Understanding and interpreting video content.

By leveraging the power of CNNs, we can build intelligent systems capable of performing complex visual tasks with high accuracy.

- **Recurrent Neural Networks (RNNs):** Process sequential data like text and time series.

Recurrent Neural Networks (RNNs) are specifically designed to handle sequential data, where the order of information matters. Unlike feedforward neural networks, RNNs have internal memory that allows them to process information over time.

Core Concept of RNNs:

- **Recurrent connections:** Information is passed from one step of the network to the next, creating a loop or cycle.
- **Hidden state:** This internal memory stores information about past inputs.
- **Time steps:** The network processes data sequentially, one time step at a time.

Challenges with Standard RNNs:

- **Vanishing gradient problem:** Difficulty in learning long-term dependencies.

Improvements: Long Short-Term Memory (LSTM) and Gated Recurrent Unit (GRU)

- **LSTM:** Introduces gates (input, forget, output) to control the flow of information, mitigating the vanishing gradient problem.
- **GRU:** Simplified version of LSTM with fewer parameters, often achieving comparable performance.

Applications of RNNs:

- **Natural Language Processing (NLP):** Language modeling, machine translation, text summarization, sentiment analysis.
- **Time Series Analysis:** Stock price prediction, weather forecasting, anomaly detection.
- **Speech Recognition:** Converting audio into text.
- **Handwriting Recognition:** Recognizing handwritten text.

By understanding the architecture and capabilities of RNNs, you can effectively tackle a wide range of sequential data problems.

- **Long Short-Term Memory (LSTM):** A type of RNN capable of learning long-term dependencies.

Long Short-Term Memory (LSTM): Mastering Long-Term Dependencies

Long Short-Term Memory (LSTM) is a specialized type of Recurrent Neural Network (RNN) designed to address the vanishing gradient problem and effectively capture long-term dependencies in sequential data.

Key Components of LSTM:

- **Cell state:** Stores information over long periods, acting as a conveyor belt.
- **Input gate:** Controls the flow of new information into the cell state.
- **Output gate:** Determines what information from the cell state is outputted.
- **Forget gate:** Decides which information to discard from the cell state.

How LSTM Works:

1. **Input gate:** Decides which information from the input and previous hidden state should be stored in the cell state.
2. **Forget gate:** Determines which information should be removed from the cell state.
3. **Cell state update:** The cell state is updated based on the input and forget gates.
4. **Output gate:** Decides which information from the cell state should be output as the hidden state.

Advantages of LSTM:

- **Effective handling of long-term dependencies:** Retains information for extended periods.
- **Versatility:** Applicable to various sequence-based tasks.
- **Improved performance:** Often outperforms standard RNNs on challenging problems.

Applications of LSTM:

- **Natural Language Processing:** Machine translation, text summarization, sentiment analysis.
- **Time Series Analysis:** Stock price prediction, weather forecasting.
- **Speech Recognition:** Converting audio to text.
- **Anomaly Detection:** Identifying unusual patterns in sequential data.

By understanding the intricacies of LSTMs, you can effectively tackle complex sequential problems and build robust machine learning models.

- **Generative Adversarial Networks (GANs):** Generate new data instances similar to the training data.

Generative Adversarial Networks (GANs): Creating New Worlds

Generative Adversarial Networks (GANs) are a class of machine learning frameworks that pit two neural networks against each other in a competitive process. This adversarial setup drives the generation of highly realistic synthetic data.

Components of GANs:

- **Generator:** Creates new data instances from random noise.
- **Discriminator:** Evaluates the generated data and determines if it's real or fake.

How GANs Work:

1. **Generator:** Produces synthetic data based on random noise input.
2. **Discriminator:** Receives both real and generated data, aiming to classify them correctly.
3. **Adversarial training:** The generator learns to produce data that fools the discriminator, while the discriminator improves at distinguishing real and fake data.

Applications of GANs:

- **Image generation:** Creating realistic images, art, and deepfakes.
- **Video generation:** Generating videos with realistic motion and content.
- **Data augmentation:** Increasing dataset size by generating synthetic data.
- **Style transfer:** Transferring the style of one image to another.

GANs have shown remarkable capabilities in generating highly realistic and diverse data, opening up new possibilities in various fields.

Applications of Deep Learning

Deep learning has revolutionized various fields:

- **Computer Vision:** Image recognition, object detection, image generation.

Computer Vision: Seeing the World Through Machines

Computer vision is a field of artificial intelligence that enables computers to interpret and understand visual information from the world, similar to how humans do. It involves developing algorithms and techniques that allow computers to process and analyze images and videos to extract meaningful information.

Key Areas of Computer Vision:

- **Image Recognition:** Identifying and classifying objects within an image.
    - Examples: facial recognition, product categorization.
- **Object Detection:** Locating and identifying objects within an image or video.
    - Examples: self-driving cars, security surveillance.
- **Image Segmentation:** Dividing an image into different regions or objects.
    - Examples: medical image analysis, autonomous vehicles.
- **Image Generation:** Creating new images or modifying existing ones.
    - Examples: art generation, image inpainting.

Techniques and Algorithms:

- **Convolutional Neural Networks (CNNs):** The backbone of modern computer vision, excelling at feature extraction.
- **Feature Extraction:** Converting images into numerical representations for machine learning.
- **Image Preprocessing:** Enhancing image quality and preparing data for analysis.
- **Deep Learning:** Utilizing complex neural networks for advanced tasks.

Applications of Computer Vision:

- **Healthcare:** Medical image analysis, disease diagnosis, surgical assistance.
- **Automotive:** Self-driving cars, advanced driver assistance systems.
- **Retail:** Product image search, visual search, inventory management.
- **Security:** Facial recognition, surveillance, object tracking.

By understanding the fundamentals of computer vision and leveraging advanced techniques, you can build intelligent systems capable of extracting valuable insights from visual data.

- **Natural Language Processing (NLP):** Machine translation, sentiment analysis, text generation.

Natural Language Processing (NLP) is a branch of artificial intelligence that focuses on the interaction between computers and human language. It enables machines to understand, interpret, and generate human language in a way that is both meaningful and useful.

Key Areas of NLP:

- **Machine Translation:** Translating text from one language to another.
    - Examples: Google Translate, DeepL Translator.
- **Sentiment Analysis:** Determining the sentiment expressed in text (positive, negative, neutral).

- Examples: Social media monitoring, customer feedback analysis.

- **Text Generation:** Creating human-like text, such as poems, scripts, or articles.
  - Examples: Language models like GPT-3.
- **Text Summarization:** Condensing long pieces of text into shorter summaries.
- **Named Entity Recognition (NER):** Identifying and classifying named entities (persons, organizations, locations).

Challenges in NLP:

- **Ambiguity:** Natural language is often ambiguous, requiring context understanding.
- **Contextual understanding:** Capturing the nuances of language and meaning.
- **Data availability:** Access to large and diverse datasets is crucial for training models.

Techniques Used in NLP:

- **Tokenization:** Breaking text into individual words or subwords.
- **Stemming and Lemmatization:** Reducing words to their root form.
- **Part-of-speech tagging:** Assigning grammatical labels to words.
- **Dependency parsing:** Analyzing the grammatical structure of sentences.
- **Word embeddings:** Representing words as numerical vectors.

By mastering NLP techniques, you can unlock the power of human language data and build intelligent applications.

- **Speech Recognition:** Voice assistants, transcription services.

Speech recognition, also known as automatic speech recognition (ASR) or speech-to-text, is the process of converting spoken language into written text. It's a complex task that involves acoustic modeling, language modeling, and decoding.

Key Components of Speech Recognition:

- **Acoustic modeling:** Converts speech signals into acoustic features.
- **Language modeling:** Predicts the most likely sequence of words based on language rules.
- **Decoding:** Combines acoustic and language models to produce text output.

Challenges in Speech Recognition:

- **Noise:** Background noise can interfere with accurate transcription.
- **Accents and dialects:** Different speech patterns can impact recognition accuracy.
- **Homophones:** Words with similar pronunciation can lead to ambiguity.
- **Real-time processing:** Ensuring low latency for applications like voice assistants.

Applications of Speech Recognition:

- **Voice assistants:** Enabling interaction with devices through voice commands.
- **Transcription services:** Converting spoken content into written text.
- **Accessibility:** Providing speech-to-text capabilities for people with disabilities.
- **Call center automation:** Analyzing customer interactions for insights.

By leveraging advanced algorithms and techniques, speech recognition systems are becoming increasingly accurate and efficient.

- **Healthcare:** Medical image analysis, drug discovery, disease prediction.

Healthcare is one of the most impactful domains for machine learning. By leveraging vast amounts of patient data, AI can revolutionize diagnosis, treatment, and patient care.

Medical Image Analysis

- **Task:** Analyzing medical images like X-rays, MRIs, and CT scans to detect abnormalities.
- **Techniques:** Convolutional Neural Networks (CNNs), image segmentation, object detection.
- **Applications:** Cancer detection, disease diagnosis, surgical planning.

Drug Discovery

- **Task:** Identifying potential drug candidates and optimizing their properties.
- **Techniques:** Generative models, molecular simulations, reinforcement learning.
- **Applications:** Accelerating drug development, reducing costs, and improving treatment efficacy.

Disease Prediction

- **Task:** Forecasting the likelihood of a patient developing a disease based on medical history, genetic data, and lifestyle factors.
- **Techniques:** Predictive modeling, survival analysis.
- **Applications:** Early disease detection, personalized prevention strategies.

Other Applications:

- **Wearable devices:** Monitoring patient health, detecting anomalies.
- **Electronic health records (EHR) analysis:** Extracting insights from patient data for improved care.
- **Clinical decision support systems:** Providing recommendations to healthcare providers.

Machine learning has the potential to significantly improve patient outcomes, reduce healthcare costs, and accelerate medical research.

- **Autonomous Vehicles:** Image processing, object detection, decision making.

Autonomous vehicles represent a cutting-edge application of machine learning and computer vision. These vehicles rely on a complex interplay of sensors, algorithms, and computational power to navigate safely and efficiently.

Key Components of Autonomous Vehicles:

- **Perception:** Understanding the environment through sensors like cameras, lidar, radar, and ultrasonic sensors.
- **Localization:** Determining the vehicle's precise location and orientation.
- **Mapping:** Creating and updating maps of the environment.
- **Planning:** Deciding on the optimal path and maneuvers.
- **Control:** Executing the planned actions through steering, acceleration, and braking.

Machine Learning Techniques:

- **Computer Vision:** For object detection, lane detection, traffic sign recognition, and pedestrian detection.
- **Sensor Fusion:** Combining data from multiple sensors for a comprehensive understanding of the environment.
- **Path Planning:** Using algorithms like A* search or Dijkstra's algorithm to find optimal routes.
- **Control Systems:** Implementing control algorithms for steering, acceleration, and braking.
- **Deep Learning:** For complex tasks like object recognition, behavior prediction, and decision making.

Challenges in Autonomous Vehicles:

- **Safety:** Ensuring the highest level of safety for passengers and pedestrians.
- **Ethical considerations:** Making moral decisions in complex scenarios.
- **Legal and regulatory frameworks:** Developing appropriate laws and regulations.
- **Infrastructure:** Adapting roads and infrastructure for autonomous vehicles.

Autonomous vehicles represent a significant leap forward in transportation and have the potential to revolutionize urban mobility.

- **Financial Services:** Fraud detection, algorithmic trading, risk assessment.

The financial industry has undergone a significant transformation due to the integration of machine learning. Its ability to process vast amounts of data and identify patterns has led to innovative solutions and improved decision-making.

Fraud Detection

- **Anomaly detection:** Identifying unusual transaction patterns.
- **Machine learning models:** Building predictive models to flag suspicious activities.
- **Real-time monitoring:** Detecting fraud as it occurs.

Algorithmic Trading

- **High-frequency trading:** Executing large numbers of orders at high speeds.
- **Predictive modeling:** Forecasting market trends and making trading decisions.
- **Risk management:** Assessing market volatility and portfolio risk.

Risk Assessment

- **Credit scoring:** Evaluating creditworthiness of individuals and businesses.
- **Insurance underwriting:** Assessing risk profiles for insurance policies.
- **Market risk assessment:** Identifying potential financial losses.

Other Applications:

- **Customer churn prediction:** Identifying customers likely to leave.
- **Personalized financial advice:** Tailoring recommendations based on individual needs.
- **Chatbots and virtual assistants:** Providing customer support and financial guidance.

By leveraging machine learning, financial institutions can enhance efficiency, reduce risks, and improve customer experiences.

Challenges and Future Directions

Despite its successes, deep learning faces challenges such as:

- **Data Hunger:** Requires massive amounts of data for training.

Data hunger is a characteristic of many modern machine learning models, particularly deep learning models. They require vast amounts of data to learn complex patterns and make accurate predictions.

Reasons for Data Hunger:

- **Complex models:** Deep neural networks have millions of parameters that need to be tuned.
- **Real-world complexity:** Capturing the nuances of real-world data requires extensive examples.
- **Overfitting prevention:** More data helps to generalize the model and prevent overfitting.

Challenges of Data Hunger:

- **Data acquisition:** Collecting and labeling large datasets can be time-consuming and expensive.
- **Data quality:** Ensuring data accuracy, consistency, and relevance is crucial.
- **Computational resources:** Processing and storing massive datasets requires significant computing power.

Mitigating Data Hunger:

- **Data augmentation:** Creating synthetic data to expand the dataset.
- **Transfer learning:** Leveraging knowledge from pre-trained models on larger datasets.
- **Data efficiency techniques:** Developing algorithms that can learn from smaller datasets.

While data hunger is a reality in many machine learning projects, careful consideration of data acquisition, preprocessing, and model efficiency can help mitigate its impact.

- **Black Box Nature:** Difficult to interpret how the network arrives at decisions.

The **black box nature** of many machine learning models, particularly deep neural networks, poses a significant challenge. While these models often achieve exceptional performance, their decision-making processes are often opaque, making it difficult to understand how they arrive at their outputs.

Reasons for Black Box Nature:

- **Complexity:** Deep neural networks with numerous layers and parameters create intricate interactions.
- **Non-linearity:** The combination of non-linear activation functions makes it hard to trace the flow of information.
- **Feature interactions:** Complex interactions between features can be difficult to disentangle.

Implications of Black Box Models:

- **Trustworthiness:** Difficulty in explaining model decisions can erode trust.
- **Bias:** Unfair biases may be present without detection.
- **Regulations:** Industries with strict regulations require explainable models.

Addressing the Black Box Problem:

- **Model interpretability techniques:** LIME, SHAP, and other methods aim to provide insights into model decisions.
- **Feature importance:** Understanding which features contribute most to the model's output.
- **Simpler models:** Consider using more interpretable models like decision trees or linear regression.
- **Domain knowledge:** Incorporate expert knowledge to validate model decisions.

While black box models offer impressive performance, understanding their inner workings is crucial for responsible and ethical AI development.

- **Computational Cost:** Training complex models can be computationally expensive.

Computational cost is a significant challenge in machine learning, particularly when dealing with complex models and large datasets. Training these models can consume substantial computational resources, including:

- **Hardware:** High-performance GPUs, TPUs, or specialized hardware accelerators.
- **Energy consumption:** Powering these devices can be costly.
- **Time:** Training can take hours, days, or even weeks.

Factors Affecting Computational Cost:

- **Model complexity:** Larger and deeper models require more computations.
- **Dataset size:** Larger datasets demand more processing power.
- **Hyperparameter tuning:** Experimenting with different hyperparameters can be computationally expensive.
- **Batch size:** The number of samples processed at once impacts training time.

Mitigating Computational Cost:

- **Hardware optimization:** Leveraging GPUs, TPUs, or cloud-based computing resources.
- **Model optimization:** Pruning, quantization, and knowledge distillation.
- **Algorithm optimization:** Choosing efficient algorithms and data structures.
- **Hyperparameter tuning:** Efficient search strategies like Bayesian optimization.

By carefully considering these factors and implementing appropriate strategies, it's possible to manage computational costs while achieving desired model performance.

Future research focuses on:

- **Explainable AI:** Making deep learning models more interpretable.

Explainable AI (XAI) is a rapidly growing field focused on making complex machine learning models more understandable and transparent. Its goal is to bridge the gap between humans and AI, fostering trust and accountability.

Why Explainable AI Matters:

- **Trust and acceptance:** Understanding how models reach decisions builds trust.
- **Regulatory compliance:** Many industries require explainable models.
- **Error detection:** Identifying biases and errors in model outputs.
- **Model improvement:** Gaining insights into model behavior for optimization.

Key Techniques in XAI:

- **Local interpretability:** Understanding individual predictions.
  - LIME (Local Interpretable Model-Agnostic Explanations)
  - SHAP (SHapley Additive exPlanations)
- **Global interpretability:** Understanding overall model behavior.
  - Partial Dependence Plots (PDP)
  - Feature importance
- **Model simplification:** Using simpler models for better interpretability (e.g., decision trees).

Challenges in XAI:

- **Trade-off between explainability and accuracy:** Simpler models might be more interpretable but less accurate.
- **Complex interactions:** Understanding how features interact can be challenging.
- **User understanding:** Effectively communicating complex explanations to non-technical audiences.

By prioritizing explainability, we can create AI systems that are not only powerful but also trustworthy and responsible.

- **Efficient Deep Learning:** Developing algorithms and hardware for faster training.

Efficient deep learning is crucial for handling complex models and large datasets within reasonable timeframes. It involves a combination of algorithmic optimizations and hardware acceleration.

Algorithmic Optimizations:

- **Model architecture:** Designing efficient network structures (e.g., MobileNet, EfficientNet).
- **Hyperparameter tuning:** Finding optimal hyperparameters for faster convergence.
- **Optimizer selection:** Choosing efficient optimization algorithms (e.g., Adam, RMSprop).
- **Batch size:** Experimenting with different batch sizes to balance memory usage and training speed.
- **Learning rate scheduling:** Dynamically adjusting learning rate during training.

Hardware Acceleration:

- **GPUs:** Leveraging parallel processing capabilities for matrix operations.
- **TPUs:** Specialized hardware designed for machine learning workloads.
- **FPGA:** Reconfigurable hardware for custom acceleration.
- **Cloud computing:** Accessing high-performance computing resources on demand.

Other Considerations:

- **Distributed training:** Distributing computations across multiple devices.
- **Mixed precision training:** Using lower precision data types to reduce memory footprint.
- **Model compression:** Reducing model size for faster inference.
- **Quantization:** Reducing numerical precision to accelerate computations.

By combining these techniques, it's possible to significantly reduce training and inference times while maintaining model performance.

- **Transfer Learning:** Leveraging knowledge from one task to improve performance on another.

Transfer learning is a machine learning technique where a model trained on one task is reused as the starting point for a model on a second related task. It's a powerful approach to address challenges related to data scarcity and computational resources.

Key Concepts in Transfer Learning:

- **Pre-trained model:** A model trained on a large dataset for a specific task (e.g., ImageNet for image classification).
- **Fine-tuning:** Adapting the pre-trained model to a new task by retraining the final layers or some of the earlier layers.
- **Feature extraction:** Using the pre-trained model to extract features from new data and training a new classifier on top.

Benefits of Transfer Learning:

- **Improved performance:** Leveraging knowledge from a large dataset.
- **Faster training:** Reducing training time compared to training from scratch.
- **Reduced data requirements:** Achieving good results with smaller datasets.

Applications of Transfer Learning:

- **Computer vision:** Transferring knowledge from ImageNet to classify medical images.
- **Natural language processing:** Using pre-trained language models for sentiment analysis or text classification.
- **Other domains:** Transfer learning can be applied to various fields with limited data.

By effectively utilizing transfer learning, you can accelerate model development and achieve better performance, especially when dealing with limited data resources.

- Model Selection and Evaluation: Picking the Best Model for the Job

Model selection and evaluation is a critical phase in the machine learning pipeline. It involves choosing the most suitable model from a pool of candidates and assessing its performance on unseen data. This process ensures that the deployed model is not only accurate but also reliable and generalizable.

Understanding the Process

1. **Define the Problem:** Clearly articulate the problem you're trying to solve. Is it a classification, regression, clustering, or another type of problem?
2. **Data Preparation:** Ensure your data is clean, preprocessed, and suitable for modeling. Handle missing values, outliers, and feature scaling appropriately.
3. **Model Selection:** Choose a set of potential models based on the problem type and data characteristics. This might include linear regression, logistic regression, decision trees, random forests, support vector machines, neural networks, and more.
4. **Hyperparameter Tuning:** Optimize the parameters of each model using techniques like grid search, random search, or Bayesian optimization.
5. **Model Evaluation:** Assess the performance of the tuned models using appropriate metrics.
6. **Model Comparison:** Compare the performance of different models to select the best one.
7. **Model Deployment:** Deploy the chosen model into a production environment.

Key Evaluation Metrics

The choice of evaluation metrics depends on the problem type. Some common metrics include:

- **Classification:** Accuracy, precision, recall, F1-score, confusion matrix, ROC curve, AUC
- **Regression:** Mean squared error (MSE), mean absolute error (MAE), R-squared
- **Clustering:** Silhouette coefficient, Calinski-Harabasz index, Davies-Bouldin index

Model Selection Techniques

- **Holdout Method:** Split the data into training and testing sets.
- **Cross-Validation:** Divide the data into k folds, train on k-1 folds, and test on the remaining fold. Repeat k times.
- **Hyperparameter Tuning:** Optimize model parameters using techniques like grid search, random search, or Bayesian optimization.

Challenges and Considerations

- **Overfitting:** Occurs when a model performs well on training data but poorly on new data.
- **Underfitting:** Occurs when a model is too simple to capture the underlying patterns in the data.
- **Imbalanced Dataset:** If classes are imbalanced, accuracy might be misleading. Consider using precision, recall, or F1-score.
- **Computational Cost:** Some models are computationally expensive to train and evaluate.
- **Interpretability:** Some models (e.g., decision trees) are more interpretable than others (e.g., deep neural networks).

Example: Choosing a Model for Credit Card Fraud Detection

- **Problem type:** Binary classification (fraudulent or not)
- **Data:** Imbalanced dataset with numerical and categorical features
- **Models:** Logistic regression, random forest, support vector machine, and neural network
- **Evaluation metrics:** Precision, recall, F1-score, ROC curve, AUC
- **Considerations:** Handle class imbalance, optimize for precision or recall based on business requirements, consider interpretability for explainability.

Additional Tips

- Start with simple models and gradually increase complexity.
- Experiment with different feature engineering techniques.
- Use ensemble methods to combine multiple models.
- Regularly monitor model performance in production.

By carefully selecting and evaluating models, you can build robust and effective machine learning systems.

Feature Engineering:

Feature engineering is the art and science of transforming raw data into meaningful features that can be used as input to machine learning algorithms. It's often considered the most crucial step in the machine learning pipeline, as the quality of features significantly impacts model performance.

Why is Feature Engineering Important?

- **Improved Model Performance:** Well-engineered features can boost accuracy, precision, recall, and other metrics.
- **Enhanced Interpretability:** Meaningful features can help understand the model's decision-making process.
- **Reduced Data Complexity:** Feature engineering can simplify complex data, making it easier for models to learn.

Key Feature Engineering Techniques

1. Data Imputation:

- Handling missing values using techniques like mean/median imputation, mode imputation, or more sophisticated methods like KNN imputation.

2. Data Scaling:

- Normalizing or standardizing numerical features to ensure they have a similar scale, preventing features with larger values from dominating the model.

3. Categorical Encoding:

- Converting categorical data into numerical format using techniques like one-hot encoding, label encoding, or target encoding.

4. Feature Transformation:

- Applying mathematical transformations to features to improve their distribution or relationship with the target variable.

Common transformations include log, square root, and normalization.

5. Feature Creation:

- Generating new features by combining existing ones or extracting information from raw data. Examples include:
    - Polynomial features
    - Interaction features
    - Date and time features
    - Textual features (e.g., TF-IDF)

6. Feature Selection:

- Identifying the most relevant features and discarding irrelevant ones to improve model efficiency and performance. Techniques include correlation analysis, feature importance, and dimensionality reduction.

Example: Predicting House Prices

- **Raw data:** Number of bedrooms, square footage, location, age of the house, etc.
- **Feature engineering:**
    - Create new features like price per square foot, number of bathrooms, and age category.
    - Encode categorical features like location into numerical representations.
    - Scale numerical features like square footage.

- ◦ Select the most important features using correlation analysis or feature importance.

Challenges and Best Practices

- **Domain Expertise:** Understanding the problem domain is crucial for effective feature engineering.
- **Iterative Process:** Feature engineering is often an iterative process, requiring experimentation and refinement.
- **Balancing Complexity and Performance:** Avoid creating overly complex features that might lead to overfitting.
- **Visualization:** Use data visualization to explore relationships between features and the target variable.

CHAPTER EIGHT

Defining Your Project

The foundation of any successful machine learning project lies in clearly defining the problem and acquiring relevant data. This initial phase sets the stage for the entire project.

Choosing a Problem

A well-defined problem is the cornerstone of a successful project. Consider the following steps:

1. **Identify a Problem:** Look for areas where data-driven solutions can create value. This could be in business, healthcare, finance, or any other domain.
2. **Define the Problem Clearly:** Clearly articulate the problem you're trying to solve. What is the desired outcome?
3. **Consider Feasibility:** Evaluate the availability of data and resources required to tackle the problem.

   Example:

- **Problem:** Customer churn prediction for a telecommunications company.
- **Goal:** Identify customers at risk of leaving to implement retention strategies.

Gathering Data

Data is the fuel for machine learning models. Key considerations:

1. **Data Relevance:** Ensure the data is directly related to the problem you're trying to solve.
2. **Data Quality:** Assess data for accuracy, completeness, and consistency.
3. **Data Quantity:** Determine the required data volume for your model.
4. **Data Sources:** Identify potential data sources (internal databases, public datasets, APIs, etc.).
5. **Data Collection Methods:** Choose appropriate methods (surveys, web scraping, sensors, etc.).
6. **Data Preprocessing:** Clean, transform, and prepare data for modeling.

   Example:

- **Data sources:** Customer demographics, usage patterns, billing information, customer support interactions.
- **Data preprocessing:** Handle missing values, normalize numerical features, encode categorical features.

Common Challenges and Solutions

- **Data Scarcity:** Explore data augmentation techniques, transfer learning, or synthetic data generation.
- **Data Quality Issues:** Implement data cleaning and validation processes.
- **Data Privacy:** Adhere to data protection regulations (GDPR, CCPA, etc.).

Key Considerations

- **Problem Framing:** Clearly define the problem and desired outcome.
- **Data Requirements:** Identify the necessary data types and sources.
- **Data Quality:** Ensure data accuracy and completeness.
- **Ethical Considerations:** Be mindful of data privacy and bias.

By carefully selecting a problem and gathering high-quality data, you lay a strong foundation for your machine learning project.

Would you like to explore a specific problem or data collection challenge?

For instance, we could discuss:

- How to identify a promising problem area
- Techniques for data cleaning and preprocessing
- Ethical considerations in data collection

Implementing Your Model:

Once you've meticulously crafted your model, the next crucial step is to deploy it into a real-world environment. This process involves translating your theoretical model into a practical application.

Key Stages of Model Implementation

1. **Model Selection and Training:**

    - Choose the optimal model based on evaluation metrics.
    - Retrain the model on the entire dataset for final deployment.

2. **Model Deployment:**
    - Choose a suitable deployment platform (cloud, on-premises, edge).
    - Create a robust infrastructure to handle model serving.
    - Develop APIs for model interaction.
    - Implement version control for model updates.
3. **Model Monitoring:**
    - Continuously track model performance in production.
    - Detect concept drift and data quality issues.
    - Implement retraining and redeployment mechanisms.

Challenges and Considerations

- **Model Performancc Drift:** Over time, model performance can degrade due to changes in data distribution.
- **Scalability:** Ensure the model can handle increased data volume and traffic.
- **Explainability:** Understand the model's decision-making process for regulatory compliance and trust.
- **Data Privacy:** Protect sensitive data during model deployment and usage.

Best Practices

- **Model Retraining:** Regularly update the model with new data to maintain performance.
- **A/B Testing:** Compare the performance of different model versions.

- **Error Analysis:** Analyze model errors to identify areas for improvement.
- **Continuous Monitoring:** Track key performance indicators (KPIs) and set up alerts for anomalies.

Example: Implementing a Fraud Detection Model

- **Deployment:** Deploy the model as a microservice on a cloud platform.
- **Monitoring:** Track fraud detection rates, false positive rates, and model latency.
- **Retraining:** Re-train the model with new fraud patterns to improve accuracy.

Tools and Technologies

- **Cloud platforms:** AWS, GCP, Azure
- **Model serving frameworks:** TensorFlow Serving, TorchServe, MLflow
- **Containerization:** Docker, Kubernetes
- **Monitoring tools:** Prometheus, Grafana

By following these guidelines and leveraging appropriate tools, you can successfully transition your model from a research project to a valuable production system.

- Deployment and Beyond: Sharing Your Work and Continuous Improvement

Deployment and Beyond: Sharing Your Work and Continuous Improvement

Once your model is deployed, the journey doesn't end. It's the beginning of a new phase: sharing your work, gathering feedback, and continuously improving your model.

Sharing Your Work

- **Publication:** Consider publishing your work in academic journals or conferences to contribute to the field.
- **Open Source:** Share your code and model on platforms like GitHub for collaboration and community engagement.
- **Presentations:** Present your findings at industry events, meetups, or webinars.

Gathering Feedback

- **User Feedback:** Collect feedback from users to understand how the model is performing in real-world conditions.
- **Expert Review:** Seek input from domain experts to identify potential improvements.
- **Competitions:** Participate in machine learning competitions to benchmark your model against others.

Continuous Improvement

- **Model Retraining:** Update your model with new data to maintain performance.

- **Hyperparameter Tuning:** Fine-tune model parameters for better results.
- **Feature Engineering:** Explore new features to enhance model accuracy.
- **Algorithm Selection:** Experiment with different algorithms to find the best fit.

MLOps (Machine Learning Operations)

MLOps is a set of practices that aims to deploy and maintain machine learning models in production reliably and efficiently. Key components include:

- **Continuous Integration and Continuous Delivery (CI/CD):** Automate the build, test, and deployment process.

Understanding CI/CD

CI/CD is a methodology that automates the build, test, and deployment process of software applications. It's a cornerstone of modern software development, particularly in DevOps environments.

Continuous Integration (CI)

- **Frequent integration:** Developers merge their code changes into a shared repository multiple times a day.
- **Automated build and testing:** Every code change triggers an automated build and test process.
- **Early detection of issues:** Problems are identified quickly, reducing integration challenges and improving code quality.

Continuous Delivery (CD)

- **Automated deployment:** Code changes that pass tests are automatically deployed to a staging or production environment.
- **Manual or automated release:** The final step to production can be manual or automated based on business requirements.
- **Faster time-to-market:** Reduces the time it takes to get new features or bug fixes into the hands of users.

Benefits of CI/CD

- **Improved software quality:** Early detection of defects, increased test coverage.
- **Faster time-to-market:** Reduced deployment time, increased release frequency.
- **Enhanced collaboration:** Better communication and teamwork among development and operations teams.
- **Increased efficiency:** Automation of repetitive tasks, freeing up developers to focus on higher-value work.
- **Reduced risk:** Early detection of issues minimizes the impact of failures.

Key Components of a CI/CD Pipeline

A CI/CD pipeline is a series of automated steps that transform code from development to deployment.

- **Version control:** Manages code changes (Git, SVN).
- **Build server:** Compiles code into executable artifacts (Jenkins, GitLab CI/CD, CircleCI).
- **Test automation:** Executes tests to ensure code quality (JUnit, Selenium).
- **Deployment automation:** Deploys applications to different environments (Kubernetes, Docker).

- **Monitoring and logging:** Tracks application performance and identifies issues (Prometheus, Grafana).

Example CI/CD Workflow

1. A developer commits code changes to a shared repository.
2. The CI server detects the change and triggers a build.
3. The build process compiles the code, runs unit tests, and creates a deployable artifact.
4. If tests pass, the artifact is deployed to a staging environment.
5. Manual or automated testing is performed in the staging environment.
6. If the application passes all tests, it is deployed to production.

Best Practices for CI/CD

- **Small, frequent code commits:** Limit the scope of changes to reduce integration issues.
- **Automated testing at all levels:** Unit, integration, and end-to-end tests are essential.
- **Infrastructure as code:** Manage infrastructure using code for consistency and reproducibility.
- **Continuous monitoring:** Track application performance and identify issues early.
- **Collaboration between teams:** Effective communication is crucial for CI/CD success.

By implementing CI/CD, organizations can significantly improve their software development processes, leading to faster delivery, higher quality, and increased customer satisfaction.

Experiment Tracking: The Backbone of Reproducible ML

Experiment tracking is the systematic recording and management of metadata associated with machine learning experiments. It's a critical component of the modern machine learning development lifecycle, ensuring reproducibility, collaboration, and efficient model iteration.

Why Experiment Tracking Matters

- **Reproducibility:** Accurately recreate experiments to validate results and build upon previous work.
- **Efficiency:** Quickly compare experiment results, identify trends, and optimize hyperparameters.
- **Collaboration:** Share insights and findings with team members.
- **Debugging:** Easily pinpoint issues and errors by analyzing experiment history.

Key Components of Experiment Tracking

- **Metadata:** Information about the experiment, including:
    - Hyperparameters
    - Code versions
    - Data versions
    - Metrics
    - Artifacts (models, visualizations)
    - Environment details (hardware, software)

- **Organization:** Effective structuring of experiments for easy search and comparison.
- **Visualization:** Tools for visualizing experiment results and trends.

Benefits of Using Experiment Tracking Tools

- **Centralized repository:** All experiment data in one place.
- **Automated logging:** Capture essential metadata without manual effort.
- **Rich visualization:** Gain insights through interactive charts and graphs.
- **Collaboration features:** Share experiments and collaborate with team members.

Popular Experiment Tracking Tools

- **MLflow:** Open-source platform for managing the ML lifecycle.
- **Weights & Biases:** Cloud-based platform with a focus on visualization and collaboration.
- **Neptune.ai:** Designed for ML teams, offering advanced features for tracking, comparison, and collaboration.
- **TensorBoard:** Integrated with TensorFlow, provides visualization tools for ML experiments.
- **Comet.ml:** Cloud-based platform with a strong focus on experimentation and reproducibility.

Best Practices for Experiment Tracking

- **Define metadata:** Clearly specify the information to track for each experiment.
- **Version control code and data:** Ensure reproducibility by tracking code and data versions.
- **Organize experiments:** Use tags, projects, or other structures to categorize experiments.
- **Visualize results:** Use charts and graphs to understand experiment performance.
- **Collaborate effectively:** Share experiments and insights with team members.

Example Experiment Tracking Workflow

1. **Define experiment:** Set hyperparameters, data splits, and other parameters.
2. **Run experiment:** Execute the training script.
3. **Log metadata:** Record hyperparameters, metrics, and artifacts using the experiment tracking tool.
4. **Compare results:** Analyze experiment results, visualize metrics, and compare with other experiments.
5. **Iterate:** Adjust hyperparameters, data, or model architecture based on results.

By effectively utilizing experiment tracking, data scientists and ML engineers can accelerate their research, improve model performance, and build more reliable and reproducible machine learning systems.

Model Registry:

A **model registry** is a repository designed to store, version, and manage trained machine learning models. It serves as a central hub for the entire model lifecycle, from development to deployment and retirement.

Key Functions of a Model Registry

- **Model Storage:** Stores trained models in various formats (e.g., TensorFlow, PyTorch, ONNX).
- **Version Control:** Tracks different versions of a model, enabling rollback and comparison.
- **Metadata Management:** Stores essential information about models, including hyperparameters, metrics, training data, and deployment details.
- **Model Lifecycle Management:** Supports model promotion, staging, and retirement processes.
- **Model Deployment:** Integrates with deployment pipelines to deploy models to different environments.
- **Collaboration:** Enables teams to share and collaborate on models.

Benefits of Using a Model Registry

- **Improved Model Management:** Centralized storage and versioning for efficient organization.
- **Enhanced Reproducibility:** Accurate tracking of model development process.
- **Accelerated Deployment:** Streamlined model deployment to production.
- **Model Governance:** Ensures compliance and regulatory requirements.
- **Facilitated Collaboration:** Enables seamless sharing and collaboration among teams.

Popular Model Registry Tools

- **MLflow:** Open-source platform for managing the ML lifecycle, including model registry.
- **Amazon SageMaker Model Registry:** Cloud-based service for storing and managing models.
- **Google Cloud Vertex AI Model Registry:** Managed service for storing and versioning models.
- **Azure ML Model Management:** Part of the Azure ML service for model lifecycle management.
- **Weights & Biases:** Comprehensive platform for experiment tracking and model management.

Best Practices for Model Registry

- **Comprehensive Metadata:** Capture essential information about models, including hyperparameters, metrics, and training data.
- **Robust Version Control:** Implement effective versioning strategies to track model evolution.
- **Secure Storage:** Protect sensitive model information with appropriate security measures.
- **Integration with CI/CD:** Integrate the model registry into the CI/CD pipeline for automated deployment.
- **Regular Auditing:** Monitor model performance and health to ensure quality.

By effectively utilizing a model registry, organizations can streamline their ML workflows, improve model management, and accelerate time-to-market for ML-powered applications.

Monitoring and Alerting:

Monitoring and alerting are crucial components of a robust machine learning system. They ensure that models continue to perform as expected in production and promptly notify stakeholders of any issues.

Why Monitoring and Alerting Matter

- **Early Detection:** Identifies performance degradation or unexpected behavior before it impacts users.
- **Proactive Maintenance:** Enables timely model retraining or updates to address issues.
- **Risk Mitigation:** Prevents financial losses or reputational damage due to model failures.
- **Performance Optimization:** Provides insights for improving model accuracy and efficiency.

Key Components of Monitoring and Alerting

- **Metrics:** Quantifiable measures of model performance, such as accuracy, precision, recall, F1-score, and latency.
- **Data Drift:** Tracking changes in the distribution of input data over time.
- **Concept Drift:** Detecting changes in the underlying relationship between input data and target variable.
- **Model Performance Degradation:** Monitoring key performance metrics for signs of decline.
- **Alerting:** Configuring thresholds and notifications for critical events.

Challenges in Monitoring and Alerting

- **Data Volume:** Handling large amounts of data generated by models in production.
- **Metric Selection:** Choosing the right metrics to monitor model performance.
- **Alert Fatigue:** Avoiding overwhelming teams with excessive alerts.
- **Root Cause Analysis:** Determining the underlying cause of performance issues.

Best Practices for Monitoring and Alerting

- **Define Key Metrics:** Identify the most important metrics for your model and business objectives.
- **Establish Baselines:** Set performance benchmarks to compare against future results.
- **Implement Alert Thresholds:** Configure alerts for significant deviations from expected behavior.
- **Leverage Visualization:** Use dashboards to visualize model performance and identify trends.
- **Automate Response:** Create automated workflows to handle common issues.
- **Continuous Improvement:** Regularly review monitoring and alerting strategies.

Tools and Platforms

- **Cloud Platforms:** AWS CloudWatch, GCP Cloud Monitoring, Azure Monitor

- **Open-Source Solutions:** Prometheus, Grafana, ELK Stack
- **Specialized ML Monitoring Platforms:** Evidently AI, WhyLabs, Neptune.ai

Example Monitoring and Alerting Workflow

1. **Collect Metrics:** Gather data on model performance, data drift, and other relevant metrics.
2. **Analyze Metrics:** Compare current performance to baseline and identify anomalies.
3. **Trigger Alerts:** Send notifications for critical issues, such as performance drops or data drift.
4. **Investigate Issues:** Conduct root cause analysis to understand the problem.
5. **Take Action:** Retrain model, update data, or implement other corrective measures.

By effectively implementing monitoring and alerting, organizations can ensure the reliability and effectiveness of their machine learning models.

Ethical Considerations

- **Bias:** Evaluate your model for biases and mitigate them.

Bias in machine learning models is a critical issue that can lead to unfair and discriminatory outcomes. It occurs when a model learns patterns from biased data, resulting in predictions that unfairly favor or disadvantage certain groups.

Identifying Bias

The first step in mitigating bias is to identify it. Here are some common methods:

- **Data Analysis:** Examine the dataset for imbalances, underrepresentation, or overrepresentation of specific groups.
- **Model Evaluation:** Assess the model's performance across different subgroups to identify disparities.
- **Sensitivity Testing:** Deliberately modify input data to observe how the model's output changes.

Types of Bias

- **Representation Bias:** Occurs when the training data does not accurately reflect the real-world population.
- **Measurement Bias:** Inaccurate or biased data collection methods can introduce bias.
- **Algorithmic Bias:** The model's algorithm itself can introduce bias, such as favoring certain features or outcomes.
- **Confirmation Bias:** Developers may unintentionally select data or metrics that confirm their existing beliefs.

Mitigating Bias

Once bias is identified, several strategies can be employed to mitigate it:

- **Data Quality Improvement:**
    - Collect more diverse and representative data.
    - Clean and preprocess data to remove biases.
    - Resample or reweight data to balance representation.

- **Algorithm Selection:**
    - Choose algorithms less prone to bias.
    - Experiment with different algorithms and hyperparameters.
- **Fairness Metrics:**
    - Use fairness metrics to evaluate the model's performance across different groups.
    - Examples include demographic parity, equalized odds, and predictive parity.
- **Post-processing:**
    - Adjust model predictions to reduce disparities.
    - Use techniques like calibration or thresholding.
- **Regular Monitoring:**
    - Continuously monitor model performance for emerging biases.
    - Retrain models regularly to adapt to changing data distributions.

Tools and Techniques

- **Fairness libraries:** Many machine learning frameworks offer built-in fairness metrics and tools.
- **Bias detection tools:** Specialized tools can help identify biases in data and models.
- **Explainable AI:** Understanding how a model makes decisions can help uncover biases.

Example: Facial Recognition

Facial recognition systems have been shown to have biases against certain ethnic groups. To mitigate this:

- **Diverse datasets:** Include images of people from various backgrounds and demographics.
- **Fairness metrics:** Evaluate the model's accuracy across different racial and ethnic groups.
- **Adversarial testing:** Test the model with images that are intentionally manipulated to exploit biases.

Fairness in Machine Learning:

Fairness in machine learning is the crucial aspect of ensuring that a model treats all users equitably without discrimination or bias. It's essential to prevent harmful societal impacts and maintain trust in AI systems.

Key Fairness Metrics

To measure fairness, various metrics are used:

- **Demographic parity:** Ensures that the proportion of a protected attribute (e.g., race, gender) is the same in both the positive and negative predicted groups.
- **Equalized odds:** Requires both true positive rates and false positive rates to be equal across different groups.
- **Predictive parity:** Focuses on ensuring that the positive prediction rate is the same across groups.

Challenges in Achieving Fairness

- **Defining fairness:** Determining the appropriate fairness metric can be complex, as different metrics may conflict.
- **Trade-offs:** Improving fairness often involves trade-offs with other performance metrics like accuracy.
- **Data limitations:** Biased or insufficient data can hinder fairness efforts.

Strategies for Achieving Fairness

- **Data preprocessing:** Addressing imbalances and biases in the training data.
- **Fairness-aware algorithms:** Developing algorithms that explicitly consider fairness constraints.
- **Post-processing:** Adjusting model outputs to mitigate disparities.
- **Counterfactual fairness:** Identifying what would need to change in an individual's situation to achieve a different outcome.

Example:

A credit scoring model might unfairly deny loans to individuals from certain demographics. To address this:

- **Collect diverse data:** Include data from a wide range of applicants to represent different populations.
- **Use fair metrics:** Evaluate the model's performance based on demographic parity or equalized odds.
- **Implement fair algorithms:** Explore algorithms designed to minimize discriminatory outcomes.

- **Monitor for bias:** Continuously assess the model's performance to detect emerging biases.

Importance of Human-in-the-Loop

Humans play a crucial role in ensuring fairness. This includes:

- **Data curation:** Selecting and preparing data to minimize biases.
- **Model evaluation:** Assessing the model's fairness and identifying potential issues.
- **Ethical considerations:** Ensuring that fairness aligns with societal values and legal requirements.

By prioritizing fairness in the development and deployment of machine learning models, we can create AI systems that benefit everyone without perpetuating harmful biases.

Transparency in Machine Learning:

Transparency, often referred to as explainability, is crucial for understanding and trusting machine learning models. It involves making the model's decision-making process comprehensible to humans.

Why Transparency Matters

- **Trust:** Building trust between users and the model.
- **Accountability:** Identifying and rectifying biases or errors.
- **Regulation:** Adhering to regulatory requirements for explainable AI.
- **Understanding:** Gaining insights into how the model works.

Techniques for Explaining Models

- **Feature Importance:** Identifying the features that contribute most to the model's prediction.
- **Local Explanations:** Understanding how a specific prediction was made.
- **Global Explanations:** Providing a general overview of how the model works.
- **Counterfactual Explanations:** Showing what would need to change in the input to change the output.

Challenges in Achieving Transparency

- **Model Complexity:** Many modern models, like deep neural networks, are inherently complex.
- **Interpretability Trade-off:** Increasing transparency might decrease model performance.
- **Data Privacy:** Protecting sensitive information while providing explanations can be challenging.

Tools and Techniques

- **LIME (Local Interpretable Model-Agnostic Explanations):** Approximates the complex model with a simpler, more interpretable model locally.
- **SHAP (SHapley Additive exPlanations):** Attributes the prediction to each feature based on game theory.
- **Decision Trees:** Naturally interpretable models, though they might not achieve the same accuracy as complex models.

Example: Credit Scoring

A credit scoring model can use feature importance to show which factors (e.g., income, debt-to-income ratio) contribute most to the decision. Local explanations can reveal why a specific loan application was approved or denied.

Privacy:

Privacy is paramount in the age of data-driven applications. Protecting user data and complying with regulations is essential for building trust and avoiding legal repercussions.

Key Privacy Principles

- **Data Minimization:** Collect only necessary data.
- **Purpose Limitation:** Use data only for specified purposes.
- **Data Accuracy:** Ensure data is accurate and up-to-date.
- **Data Integrity:** Protect data from unauthorized access, modification, or disclosure.
- **Accountability:** Be responsible for data processing activities.

Privacy Regulations

Organizations must adhere to various privacy laws and regulations, including:

- **GDPR (General Data Protection Regulation):** EU-wide regulation governing the processing of personal data.
- **CCPA (California Consumer Privacy Act):** US state law providing consumers with privacy rights.

- **HIPAA (Health Insurance Portability and Accountability Act):** US federal law protecting health information.
- **PCI DSS (Payment Card Industry Data Security Standard):** Protects cardholder data.

Privacy-Preserving Techniques

- **Data Anonymization:** Removing identifying information from data.
- **Data Pseudonymization:** Replacing identifying information with unique identifiers.
- **Data Encryption:** Protecting data with cryptographic methods.
- **Differential Privacy:** Adding noise to data to protect individual privacy.
- **Federated Learning:** Training models on decentralized data without sharing it.

Challenges in Privacy

- **Balancing Privacy and Utility:** Protecting privacy while maintaining model performance.
- **Evolving Regulations:** Keeping up with changing privacy laws.
- **Data Breaches:** Preventing unauthorized access to sensitive data.
- **Third-Party Risks:** Managing privacy risks when sharing data with external parties.

Best Practices

- **Privacy by Design:** Incorporate privacy considerations from the outset of development.
- **Data Protection Impact Assessments (DPIAs):** Evaluate privacy risks before processing personal data.
- **User Consent:** Obtain clear and informed consent for data processing.
- **Data Subject Rights:** Implement procedures to handle data subject requests (e.g., access, rectification, erasure).
- **Employee Training:** Educate employees about privacy responsibilities.
- **Incident Response Plan:** Have a plan for responding to data breaches.

By prioritizing privacy and complying with regulations, organizations can build trust with users, mitigate risks, and protect their reputation.

Beyond the Model

- **Business Impact:** Measure the impact of your model on the organization's goals.

Business impact is the ultimate measure of a machine learning model's success. It quantifies how the model contributes to an organization's overall goals and objectives.

Key Metrics for Business Impact

To measure business impact, you need to align your model's performance with the organization's strategic objectives. Here are some key metrics to consider:

- **Financial metrics:** Revenue growth, cost reduction, profit margin, ROI.

- **Operational metrics:** Efficiency improvements, process optimization, time savings.
- **Customer-centric metrics:** Customer satisfaction, churn reduction, customer acquisition cost.
- **Market metrics:** Market share, customer lifetime value, brand reputation.

Aligning Model Outputs with Business Goals

- **Clear objectives:** Define specific, measurable, achievable, relevant, and time-bound (SMART) goals.
- **Key performance indicators (KPIs):** Identify the KPIs that directly correlate with business objectives.
- **Model evaluation:** Assess the model's performance against these KPIs.
- **Return on investment (ROI):** Calculate the financial benefits of the model.

Example: Fraud Detection Model

If a fraud detection model is implemented in a financial institution, the business impact can be measured by:

- **Reduction in fraudulent transactions:** This directly impacts financial losses.
- **Improved customer satisfaction:** By preventing fraudulent activities, customer trust increases.
- **Operational efficiency:** Streamlined fraud investigation processes.

Challenges and Considerations

- **Data availability:** Ensure you have sufficient data to measure business impact.
- **Attribution:** Determining the exact contribution of the model to business outcomes can be challenging.
- **Long-term impact:** Some impacts may take time to materialize.
- **Organizational alignment:** Ensure the model's goals align with the overall business strategy.

Best Practices

- **Start small:** Begin with a pilot project to measure impact before scaling up.
- **Continuous monitoring:** Track the model's performance and adjust as needed.
- **Communication:** Clearly communicate the model's impact to stakeholders.
- **Iteration:** Use insights to improve the model and its business impact.

By focusing on business impact, you can demonstrate the value of your machine learning models and secure ongoing support for AI initiatives.

- **New Opportunities:** Identify new applications for the model or its underlying technology.

Identifying new applications for a machine learning model or its underlying technology is crucial for maximizing its value and driving innovation. This process involves exploring new domains, industries, or use cases where the model's capabilities can be leveraged.

Key Strategies for Discovering New Opportunities

- **Deep Dive into Model Capabilities:**
    - Understand the model's strengths, weaknesses, and limitations.
    - Analyze the model's performance on different datasets and tasks.
    - Identify potential areas for improvement or expansion.
- **Market Research and Trend Analysis:**
    - Identify emerging trends and unmet needs in various industries.
    - Explore how the model can address these challenges or opportunities.
    - Analyze competitor offerings to identify gaps in the market.
- **Cross-Functional Collaboration:**
    - Engage with experts from different departments to gain diverse perspectives.
    - Identify potential synergies between the model and existing business processes.
    - Explore opportunities for collaboration with external partners.
- **Experimentation and Prototyping:**
    - Create proof-of-concept applications to test new ideas.
    - Iterate on the model and its applications based on feedback and results.

- Embrace a culture of experimentation and innovation.

Examples of New Opportunities

- **Image recognition model:** Expanding from facial recognition to medical image analysis, object detection in autonomous vehicles, or visual search applications.
- **Natural language processing model:** Developing new applications in sentiment analysis, chatbots, language translation, or content generation.
- **Recommendation system:** Exploring new domains like personalized education, healthcare recommendations, or financial product recommendations.

Challenges and Considerations

Data Availability:

Data availability is a critical factor in the development and success of new applications. Without access to relevant, high-quality data, even the most innovative ideas can falter.

Challenges in Data Availability

- **Data Silos:** Data is often fragmented across different departments or systems, making it difficult to access and integrate.
- **Data Quality Issues:** Inconsistent data formats, missing values, and inaccuracies can hinder data analysis and model development.
- **Data Privacy Regulations:** Compliance with regulations like GDPR and CCPA can restrict data sharing and usage.
- **Data Volume and Velocity:** The sheer volume and speed of data generation can overwhelm traditional data management

systems.

Strategies to Ensure Data Availability

- **Data Governance:** Establish clear policies and procedures for data ownership, access, and quality.
- **Data Integration:** Combine data from various sources into a unified view.
- **Data Quality Management:** Implement processes to clean, validate, and enrich data.
- **Data Security:** Protect data from unauthorized access, breaches, and loss.
- **Data Storage and Management:** Choose appropriate storage solutions to handle data volume and velocity.
- **Data Sharing Platforms:** Explore platforms that facilitate secure data sharing and collaboration.
- **Data Labeling and Annotation:** Prepare data for machine learning models by labeling and annotating relevant information.
- **Data Synthesis:** Generate synthetic data to augment real-world data and address privacy concerns.

Examples of Data Availability Challenges and Solutions

- **Healthcare:** Patient data is often siloed across different healthcare providers, hindering research and personalized medicine. To address this, data sharing platforms and federated learning can be used.
- **Finance:** Financial institutions generate vast amounts of data, but extracting valuable insights requires efficient data management and analysis tools. Data warehouses and cloud-based data platforms can help.
- **Retail:** Understanding customer behavior requires access to sales data, customer demographics, and product information. Data integration and data lakes can provide a comprehensive

view of the customer.

By addressing these challenges and implementing effective data availability strategies, organizations can unlock the full potential of their data and drive innovation.

Model Adaptation:

Model adaptation is the process of modifying an existing model to perform effectively on a new or different task. It's akin to retraining a skilled worker for a new role.

Key Techniques for Model Adaptation

1. **Fine-tuning:** This involves retraining the model on a smaller dataset specific to the new task while keeping the original model's weights as a starting point. It's often used for tasks similar to the original training data.
2. **Transfer Learning:** Leveraging knowledge gained from one task to improve performance on a related task. This is especially useful when there's a shortage of data for the new task.
3. **Retraining:** Building a new model from scratch using the combined dataset of the original and new data. This is resource-intensive but can be necessary for significantly different tasks.
4. **Model Architecture Modification:** Altering the model's structure to better suit the new task. This can involve adding or removing layers, changing activation functions, or modifying hyperparameters.

Challenges and Considerations

- **Data Availability:** Sufficient and high-quality data is crucial for effective adaptation.
- **Computational Resources:** Retraining and fine-tuning can be computationally expensive.
- **Overfitting:** The risk of the model becoming too specialized to the new data and performing poorly on unseen data.

- **Domain Adaptation:** Addressing differences between the source and target domains to avoid performance degradation.

Real-world Examples

- **Image Recognition:** A model trained to recognize dogs can be adapted to recognize cats by fine-tuning on a dataset of cat images.
- **Natural Language Processing:** A language model trained on general text can be adapted to generate code by fine-tuning on code-related data.
- **Medical Image Analysis:** A model trained on chest X-rays can be adapted to detect abnormalities in brain scans through transfer learning.

By effectively adapting models, organizations can unlock new opportunities, improve efficiency, and gain a competitive edge.

Ethical Implications of Model Adaptation

Model adaptation, while powerful, introduces a new set of ethical considerations.

Potential Biases

- **Amplification of Bias:** If the original model contained biases, adapting it to a new dataset might amplify those biases.
- **Data Bias:** Bias in the new dataset can be introduced or exacerbated during the adaptation process.
- **Algorithmic Bias:** Adaptation methods themselves might introduce biases if not carefully designed.

Ethical Concerns

- **Fairness and Equity:** Ensuring the adapted model treats all users fairly without discrimination.
- **Transparency:** Understanding how the model makes decisions and the impact of adaptations on those decisions.

- **Accountability:** Identifying who is responsible for the model's actions and consequences.
- **Privacy:** Protecting user data and preventing misuse of personal information.
- **Safety:** Ensuring the adapted model does not pose risks to users or society.

Mitigating Risks

- **Bias Auditing:** Regularly assess the model for biases and take corrective actions.
- **Diverse Datasets:** Use datasets that represent a wide range of populations.
- **Ethical Guidelines:** Develop clear ethical principles for model development and adaptation.
- **Explainable AI:** Make the model's decision-making process transparent.
- **Continuous Monitoring:** Monitor the model's performance in real-world settings to identify and address issues.

By proactively addressing these ethical challenges, we can ensure that model adaptation benefits society while minimizing harm.

Resource Allocation: Prioritizing for Impact and Feasibility

Resource allocation is a critical function in any organization. It involves making strategic decisions about how to distribute limited resources to maximize business value.

Key Factors for Prioritization

To effectively allocate resources, consider the following factors:

- **Business Impact:**
    - Alignment with strategic goals: How does the opportunity contribute to the overall business strategy?

  - Revenue generation: What is the potential financial return on investment (ROI)?
  - Market potential: What is the size and growth potential of the target market?
  - Competitive advantage: Does the opportunity provide a unique advantage over competitors?

- **Feasibility:**

  - Resource availability: Do you have the necessary personnel, technology, and budget?
  - Risk assessment: What are the potential risks and challenges?
  - Timeframe: How quickly can the opportunity be implemented?
  - Technical feasibility: Is the required technology mature and available?

- **Other Considerations:**

  - Customer needs: Does the opportunity address a critical customer need?
  - Regulatory compliance: Are there any legal or regulatory hurdles?
  - Organizational culture: Does the opportunity align with the company culture and values?

Prioritization Frameworks

Several frameworks can help structure the prioritization process:

- **Weighted Scoring Model:** Assign weights to different criteria and score each opportunity based on those weights.
- **Balanced Scorecard:** Consider financial, customer, internal process, and learning and growth perspectives.

- **Opportunity Assessment Matrix:** Plot opportunities based on impact and feasibility to identify high-potential projects.
- **ROI Analysis:** Calculate the expected return on investment for each opportunity.

Resource Allocation Strategies

- **Portfolio Management:** Diversify investments across different types of projects (e.g., high-risk/high-reward, low-risk/low-reward).
- **Agile Resource Allocation:** Be flexible and adaptable to changing priorities.
- **Continuous Evaluation:** Regularly assess the performance of allocated resources and make adjustments as needed.

By carefully evaluating opportunities and aligning resource allocation with strategic objectives, organizations can maximize their chances of success.

By systematically exploring new opportunities, organizations can unlock the full potential of their machine learning models and drive sustainable growth.

- **Knowledge Transfer:** Share your knowledge with the team to build a strong ML culture.

Knowledge transfer is essential for fostering a thriving ML culture. It ensures that expertise is shared, skills are developed, and the team can collectively grow.

Effective Knowledge Transfer Strategies

- **Mentorship and Coaching:**

  - Assign experienced ML practitioners as mentors to guide new team members.
  - Provide opportunities for one-on-one coaching and feedback.
  - Foster a supportive learning environment.

- **Knowledge Sharing Platforms:**

  - Create a centralized repository for code, documentation, and best practices.
  - Encourage team members to share their knowledge through blogs, wikis, or presentations.
  - Utilize collaboration tools for real-time knowledge sharing.

- **Cross-Functional Collaboration:**

  - Promote teamwork and knowledge exchange between different ML teams.
  - Encourage collaboration with other departments to gain diverse perspectives.
  - Organize joint projects and hackathons to foster knowledge sharing.

- **Training and Development:**

  - Offer regular training sessions on new ML techniques, tools, and technologies.
  - Provide opportunities for team members to attend conferences and workshops.
  - Support continuous learning and skill development.

- **Documentation and Standardization:**

  - Create clear and consistent documentation for ML processes and pipelines.
  - Establish coding standards and best practices.

- Promote knowledge capture and sharing through templates and guidelines.

Overcoming Challenges

Time Constraints:

Time is a precious resource. Often, knowledge transfer is seen as a "nice-to-have" rather than a "must-have," leading to it being squeezed into already packed schedules.

Overcoming Time Constraints

To effectively allocate time for knowledge transfer, consider the following strategies:

- **Dedicated Knowledge Transfer Time:**
    - **Scheduled Knowledge Sharing Sessions:** Regular, recurring meetings for knowledge exchange.
    - **Mentorship Programs:** Pairing experienced employees with new hires.
    - **Cross-functional Collaboration:** Encouraging interaction between different teams.
- **Time Management Techniques:**
    - **Time Blocking:** Dedicate specific time blocks for knowledge transfer activities.
    - **Prioritization:** Identify critical knowledge areas and focus on those first.
    - **Efficiency:** Use tools and technology to streamline knowledge sharing processes.
- **Leadership Support:**

  - **Champion Knowledge Transfer:** Leaders should model the importance of knowledge sharing.
  - **Allocate Resources:** Provide necessary support, such as tools, training, and personnel.

- **Flexible Work Arrangements:**

  - **Remote Knowledge Sharing:** Utilize technology for virtual knowledge transfer.
  - **Flexible Schedules:** Allow employees to balance work and learning.

Measuring the Impact

To demonstrate the value of dedicated knowledge transfer time, track the following metrics:

- **Employee satisfaction:** Measure employee engagement and job satisfaction.
- **Knowledge retention:** Assess how well employees retain transferred knowledge.
- **Project success:**Analyze the impact of knowledge transfer on project outcomes.
- **Time-to-productivity:** Measure the time it takes new employees to become productive.

By prioritizing knowledge transfer and allocating dedicated time for it, organizations can improve efficiency, reduce errors, and foster a culture of continuous learning.

Knowledge Hoarding:

Knowledge hoarding can stifle innovation and hinder organizational growth.

A culture of openness and sharing is essential for an organization's success.

Strategies to Encourage Knowledge Sharing

1. **Leadership Buy-In:**
    - **Model the Behavior:** Leaders should openly share their knowledge and encourage others to do the same.
    - **Reward Knowledge Sharing:** Recognize and reward employees who actively share their knowledge.
2. **Create a Safe and Supportive Environment:**
    - **Open Communication:** Foster a culture of open dialogue and feedback.
    - **Psychological Safety:** Ensure employees feel comfortable sharing ideas without fear of judgment.
    - **Acknowledge Contributions:** Recognize and appreciate the value of shared knowledge.
3. **Utilize Technology:**
    - **Knowledge Management Systems:** Implement platforms for knowledge sharing and collaboration.
    - **Social Collaboration Tools:** Encourage knowledge exchange through social platforms.
    - **Learning Management Systems:** Provide a centralized repository for training materials and resources.
4. **Knowledge Sharing Initiatives:**
    - **Mentorship Programs:** Pair experienced employees with new hires.
    - **Cross-Functional Collaboration:** Encourage teamwork and knowledge exchange across departments.
    - **Knowledge Sharing Communities:** Create platforms for employees to share expertise.
5. **Measure and Reward Knowledge Sharing:**

  - **Key Performance Indicators (KPIs):** Track knowledge sharing metrics to assess effectiveness.
  - **Incentives:** Provide rewards for employees who actively contribute to knowledge sharing.

Overcoming Challenges

- **Time Constraints:** Allocate dedicated time for knowledge sharing activities.
- **Fear of Loss:** Address concerns about job security by emphasizing the benefits of collective knowledge.
- **Lack of Recognition:**

Recognize and reward knowledge sharing efforts.

- **Technical Challenges:** Provide necessary tools and training to facilitate knowledge sharing.

Skill Gaps:

Skill gaps can significantly impact an organization's performance. Addressing them requires a systematic approach.

Identifying Skill Gaps

- **Performance Reviews:**Analyze performance evaluations to identify areas where employees need improvement.
- **Employee Surveys:** Gather feedback on employees' perceived skill gaps and development needs.
- **Job Analysis:** Compare required job skills with current employee capabilities.
- **Technology Assessment:** Evaluate the organization's technological needs and employee proficiency.

Addressing Skill Gaps Through Targeted Training

- **Needs Assessment:** Clearly define the specific skills required and the target audience.
- **Learning Objectives:** Develop clear and measurable learning outcomes.
- **Training Delivery Methods:** Choose appropriate training methods (e.g., classroom, online, on-the-job).
- **Hands-on Practice:** Provide opportunities for employees to apply new skills.
- **Mentorship and Coaching:** Offer support and guidance during the learning process.
- **Performance Evaluation:** Measure training effectiveness and adjust as needed.

Additional Strategies

- **Succession Planning:** Identify potential successors and develop their skills to fill future roles.
- **Cross-Training:** Expand employees' skill sets to increase flexibility and adaptability.
- **External Partnerships:** Collaborate with educational institutions or industry experts for specialized training.
- **Employee Development Plans:** Create individualized plans to address specific skill gaps.

By proactively identifying and addressing skill gaps, organizations can build a more competent and adaptable workforce.

Language Barriers:

Language barriers can hinder effective communication and collaboration. Overcoming them requires a thoughtful approach.

Using Clear and Simple Language

- **Avoid Jargon and Technical Terms:** Use everyday language that is easily understandable.
- **Be Concise:** Get to the point without unnecessary details.

- **Provide Examples:** Illustrate complex concepts with simple examples.
- **Active Listening:** Pay attention to the listener's understanding.

Leveraging Translation Tools

- **Professional Translation:** For critical documents or communications, consider professional translators.
- **Machine Translation:** Use as a starting point, but always review and edit for accuracy.
- **Multilingual Content:** Create content in multiple languages for a wider audience.
- **Accessibility Features:** Utilize translation options and speech-to-text features in digital platforms.

Additional Considerations

- **Cultural Sensitivity:** Be aware of cultural differences in language and communication styles.
- **Non-Verbal Communication:** Use visuals, gestures, and body language to support verbal communication.
- **Patience and Understanding:** Allow extra time for communication and be patient with language learners.

By implementing these strategies, organizations can create a more inclusive environment and enhance communication across different language groups.

Measuring Knowledge Transfer Effectiveness

Assessing Knowledge Retention

Assessing knowledge retention is crucial for ensuring that training and development efforts are effective. Here are some methods:

Direct Assessment Methods

- **Knowledge Tests:** These can be pre and post-training assessments to measure knowledge gain.
- **Performance Evaluations:** Observe how well employees apply learned knowledge on the job.
- **Simulations:** Create realistic scenarios to test knowledge application under pressure.

Indirect Assessment Methods

- **Employee Surveys:** Gather feedback on the perceived value of training and how well knowledge is retained.
- **Knowledge Audits:** Evaluate the availability and accessibility of knowledge resources.
- **Turnover Analysis:**Analyze the impact of employee turnover on knowledge retention.

Key Metrics to Track

- **Knowledge Retention Rate:** Measure the percentage of information retained over time.
- **Training Return on Investment (ROI):** Calculate the financial benefits of training in relation to costs.
- **Time to Proficiency:** Assess how long it takes employees to reach a desired performance level.

Challenges and Considerations

- **Measuring Implicit Knowledge:** It can be difficult to assess tacit or unspoken knowledge.
- **Transfer of Learning:** Evaluate how well knowledge is applied to real-world situations.
- **Sustained Knowledge Retention:** Measure long-term retention to identify knowledge decay.

By combining these methods and metrics, organizations can effectively assess knowledge retention and identify areas for improvement.

Evaluating Improvement in Team Members' ML Skills

Evaluating the improvement in team members' ML skills is crucial for measuring the effectiveness of training programs and identifying areas for further development. Here are some key methods:

Direct Assessment Methods

- **Pre and Post-Training Assessments:** Compare performance on ML-related tasks before and after training.
- **Skill-Based Certifications:** Encourage team members to obtain industry-recognized certifications.
- **Coding Challenges and Competitions:** Evaluate problem-solving and coding abilities in a competitive environment.

Indirect Assessment Methods

- **Project Performance:**Analyze the quality and efficiency of ML projects before and after training.
- **Employee Surveys:** Gather feedback on perceived skill improvement and confidence levels.
- **Peer Reviews:** Encourage team members to provide feedback on each other's progress.

Specific ML Skill Areas to Evaluate

- **Theoretical Knowledge:** Understanding of ML concepts, algorithms, and techniques.
- **Practical Application:** Ability to implement ML models using programming languages like Python.
- **Data Handling:** Proficiency in data cleaning, preprocessing, and feature engineering.

- **Model Evaluation:** Skills in selecting appropriate metrics and interpreting model performance.
- **Deployment:** Knowledge of deploying ML models into production environments.

Challenges and Considerations

- **Subjectivity of Evaluation:** Some assessment methods might introduce bias.
- **Time Constraints:** Conducting thorough evaluations can be time-consuming.
- **Measuring Soft Skills:** Assessing problem-solving, creativity, and collaboration can be challenging.

By combining these methods and focusing on specific skill areas, organizations can effectively evaluate the improvement in team members' ML skills and make data-driven decisions for future development initiatives.

Measuring the Impact of Knowledge Transfer on Project Outcomes

Measuring the impact of knowledge transfer on project outcomes is crucial for demonstrating its value and identifying areas for improvement.

Key Metrics

- **Project Success Rate:** Compare the success rate of projects with and without significant knowledge transfer.
- **Project Duration:** Measure the time taken to complete projects with and without knowledge transfer.
- **Project Cost:**Analyze project costs in relation to knowledge transfer efforts.
- **Quality Metrics:** Evaluate the quality of project deliverables with and without knowledge transfer.
- **Customer Satisfaction:** Assess customer satisfaction levels based on project outcomes.

Data Collection Methods

- **Project Post-Mortems:** Conduct detailed reviews of project successes and failures.
- **Surveys and Questionnaires:** Gather feedback from project teams and stakeholders.
- **Document Analysis:** Review project plans, reports, and communication logs.
- **Financial Data:**Analyze project budgets and revenue generated.

Challenges and Considerations

- **Attribution:** Isolating the impact of knowledge transfer from other project factors can be challenging.
- **Long-Term Effects:** Measuring the full impact of knowledge transfer might require long-term analysis.
- **Qualitative Data:** Incorporating qualitative feedback can provide valuable insights.

Enhancing Knowledge Transfer Impact

- **Knowledge Sharing Platforms:** Facilitate easy access to project-related information.
- **Mentorship Programs:** Pair experienced team members with new ones.
- **Cross-Functional Collaboration:** Encourage knowledge sharing across teams.
- **Continuous Learning:** Promote a culture of continuous improvement and knowledge acquisition.

By carefully selecting metrics and using appropriate data collection methods, organizations can effectively measure the impact of knowledge transfer on project outcomes and make data-driven decisions to enhance project performance.

Assessing Team Collaboration and Knowledge Sharing

Assessing team collaboration and knowledge sharing is essential for improving team performance and fostering innovation. Here are some key methods:

Direct Assessment Methods

- **Team Surveys:** Gather feedback on team members' perceptions of collaboration and knowledge sharing.
- **Observation:** Observe team interactions during meetings, projects, and daily work.
- **Collaboration Tools Analysis:**Analyze usage patterns of collaboration tools (e.g., Slack, Microsoft Teams).

Indirect Assessment Methods

- **Project Performance:** Evaluate the impact of collaboration on project outcomes.
- **Employee Satisfaction:** Measure employee satisfaction with team dynamics and knowledge sharing.
- **Knowledge Retention:** Assess how well knowledge is shared and retained within the team.

Key Metrics

- **Collaboration Frequency:** Measure the frequency of interactions and knowledge sharing.
- **Knowledge Sharing Effectiveness:** Evaluate the impact of shared knowledge on problem-solving and decision-making.
- **Team Conflict:** Assess the level of conflict and how it is managed.
- **Team Cohesion:** Measure the level of trust and support among team members.

Challenges and Considerations

- **Subjectivity:** Team members' perceptions of collaboration can vary.
- **Data Collection:** Gathering accurate data on collaboration can be time-consuming.
- **Cultural Differences:** Collaboration styles may vary across different cultures.

By combining these methods and metrics, organizations can gain valuable insights into team collaboration and knowledge sharing, identify areas for improvement, and foster a more collaborative work environment.

By implementing effective knowledge transfer strategies, you can create a strong ML culture where everyone contributes to the team's success.

By following these steps and embracing a culture of continuous improvement, you can maximize the value of your machine learning models and drive innovation.

CHAPTER NINE

Conclusion

Machine Learning in Action: Code Your Way to Powerful Models has equipped you with the essential tools and knowledge to build effective and impactful machine learning models. By delving into the core concepts, practical implementations, and real-world applications, you've gained a solid foundation in this dynamic field.

Remember, the journey of machine learning is continuous. As technology evolves and new challenges arise, the ability to adapt and learn will be crucial. Experimentation, iteration, and a deep understanding of your data will be your guiding stars.

This book has provided you with a strong starting point, but the true potential of machine learning lies in your hands. Apply the knowledge gained to tackle complex problems, drive innovation, and create solutions that positively impact the world.

From understanding the fundamentals of supervised and unsupervised learning to mastering advanced techniques like deep learning and reinforcement learning, you've explored the breadth of machine learning possibilities. By combining theoretical knowledge with hands-on practice, you're well-prepared to build intelligent systems that drive business value and solve real-world challenges.

Now, it's time to unleash your creativity and embark on your own machine learning journey. Explore new datasets, experiment with different algorithms, and contribute to the ever-growing field of artificial intelligence.

The future of machine learning is bright, and you are part of shaping it.

CHAPTER TEN

References

1. Mohammed M, Khan MB, Bashier Mohammed BE. Machine learning: algorithms and applications. CRC Press; 2016.
2. Ardabili SF, Mosavi A, Ghamisi P, Ferdinand F, Varkonyi-Koczy AR, Reuter U, Rabczuk T, Atkinson PM. Covid-19 outbreak prediction with machine learning. Algorithms. 2020;13(10):249.
3. Baldi P. Autoencoders, unsupervised learning, and deep architectures. In: Proceedings of ICML workshop on unsupervised and transfer learning, 2012; 37–49.
4. Pedregosa F, Varoquaux G, Gramfort A, Michel V, Thirion B, Grisel O, Blondel M, Prettenhofer P, Weiss R, Dubourg V, et al. Scikit-learn: machine learning in python. J Mach Learn Res. 2011;12:2825–30.
5. Quinlan JR. C4.5: programs for machine learning. Mach Learn. 1993.
6. P.Harrington, "Machine Learning in action", Manning Publications Co., Shelter Island, New York, 2012.
7. S.Marsland, Machine learning: an algorithmic perspective. CRC press, 2015.
8. Messaoud, S.; Bradai, A.; Bukhari, S.H.R.; Quang, P.T.A.; Ahmed, O.B.; Atri, M. A survey on machine learning in internet of things: Algorithms, strategies, and applications. Internet Things 2020, 12, 100314.
9. L. Benos, *et al.*Machine learning in agriculture: a comprehensive updated review

10. Sarker, I.H. Machine Learning: Algorithms, real-world applications and research directions. SN Comput. Sci. 2021, 2, 160.
11. Yin, L.; Gao, Q.; Zhao, L.; Zhang, B.; Wang, T.; Li, S.; Liu, H. A review of machine learning for new generation smart dispatch in power systems. Eng. Appl. Artif. Intell. 2020, 88, 103372.
12. Carvalho, D.V.; Pereira, E.M.; Cardoso, J.S. Machine Learning Interpretability: A Survey on Methods and Metrics. Electronics 2019, 8, 832.
13. Verbraeken, J.; Wolting, M.; Katzy, J.; Kloppenburg, J.; Verbelen, T.; Rellermeyer, J.S. A survey on distributed machine learning. ACM Comput. Surv. 2020, 53, 1–33.
14. Pitropakis, N.; Panaousis, E.; Giannetsos, T.; Anastasiadis, E.; Loukas, G. A taxonomy and survey of attacks against machine learning. Comput. Sci. Rev. 2019, 34, 100199.
15. Choi, H.; Park, S. A Survey of Machine Learning-Based System Performance Optimization Techniques. Appl. Sci. 2021, 11, 3235.
16. Singh, A.; Thakur, N.; Sharma, A. A review of supervised machine learning algorithms. In Proceedings of the 2016 3rd International Conference on Computing for Sustainable Global Development (INDIACom), New Delhi, India, 16–18 March 2016; pp. 1310–1315.
17. Ray, S. A Quick Review of Machine Learning Algorithms. In Proceedings of the 2019 International Conference on Machine Learning, Big Data, Cloud and Parallel Computing (COMITCon), Faridabad, India, 14–16 February 2019; pp. 35–39.
18. Wu, N.; Xie, Y. A survey of machine learning for computer architecture and systems. ACM Comput. Surv. 2022, 55, 1–39.
19. Li, Z.; Yoon, J.; Zhang, R.; Rajabipour, F.; Srubar, W.V., III; Dabo, I.; Radlińska, A. Machine learning in concrete science: Applications, challenges, and best practices. NPJ Comput. Mater. 2022, 8, 127.

About Authors

Dr. K.Alice is working as Assistant Professor in Department of Computing Technologies, School of Computing, College of Engineering and Technology, SRM Institute of Science and Technology, Kattankulathur, Tamil Nadu, India. She received her Doctoral degree in Information and Communication Engineering in 2020 from Anna University, Chennai. She has presented several technical papers in National and International Conferences. She has more than 25 contributions of manuscripts in various reputed international journals to her credits. Her research interests are in Deep learning, Machine learning, Algorithm Analysis, Image processing and information Security.

Dr. Sindhuja M is working as Assistant Professor in Department of Computing Technologies, School of Computing, College of Engineering and Technology, SRM Institute of Science and Technology, Kattankulathur, Tamil Nadu, India. She received her Doctoral degree in Information and Communication Engineering in 2020 from Anna University, Chennai. She has been working in various issues of Wireless Networks domain since 2012. Her research interest includes Data Structures, WSN, IoT, Image Processing, Nature Inspired Computing, Optimization algorithms and so on. She has also published research articles in various reputed journals. She has published patents and received grants for patents on various research areas.

Dr.S.Priya is working as Assistant Professor in the Department of Computing Technologies at SRM Institute of Science and Technology. She received her Doctoral degree in Computer Science and Engineering in 2023. She obtained her Master's degree in Computer Science and Engineering from Mepco Schlenk Engineering College, Sivakasi, Tamil Nadu, India in the year 2011. She has published more than 25 articles in various reputed international journals and has published 2 patents and 1 patent grant. Her research interests include Class Imbalance Learning,

Ensemble Learning, Machine Learning and Deep Learning.

www.ingramcontent.com/pod-product-compliance
Lightning Source LLC
LaVergne TN
LVHW021154160826
845679LV00024B/2117

* 9 7 9 8 8 9 5 1 9 6 6 0 1 *